LEGENDS OF WARFARE

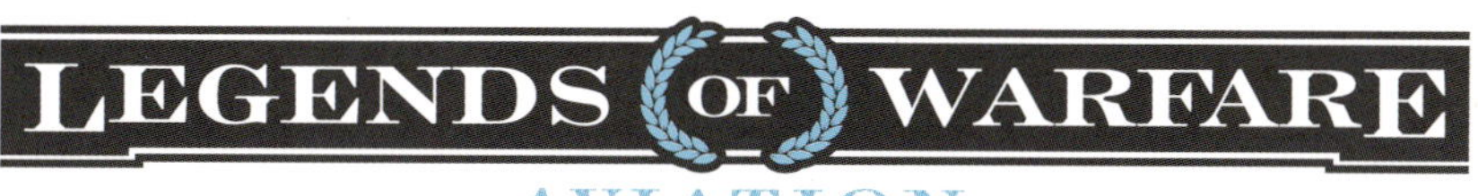

AVIATION

# CH-47 Chinook

## Boeing's Tandem-Rotor Heavy Lifter

**DAVID DOYLE**

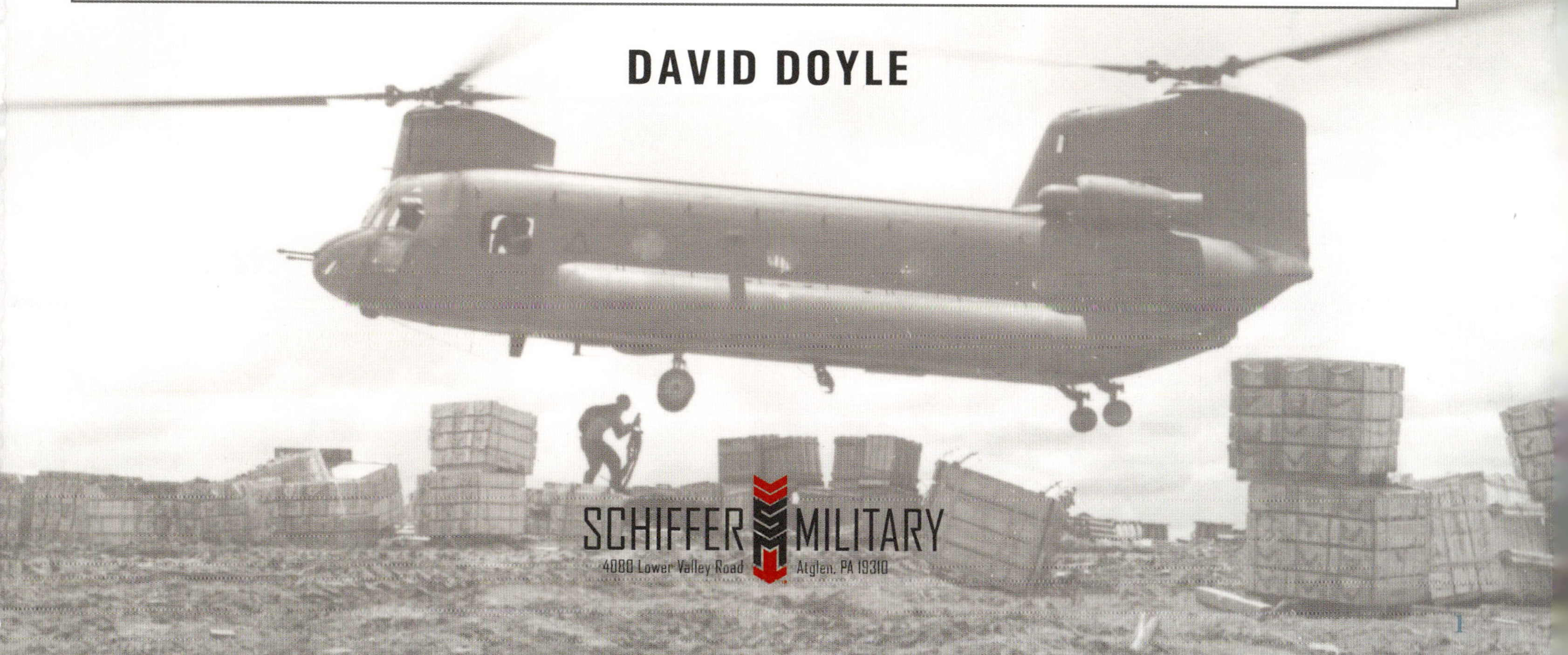

SCHIFFER MILITARY
4880 Lower Valley Road Atglen, PA 19310

Library of Congress Control Number: 2023941048



Designed by Christopher Bower
Cover design by Justin Watkinson
Type set in Impact/Minion Pro

ISBN: 978-0-7643-6785-4
Printed in India

Published by Schiffer Publishing, Ltd.
4880 Lower Valley Road
Atglen, PA 19310
Phone: (610) 593-1777; Fax: (610) 593-2002
Email: Info@schifferbooks.com
Web: www.schifferbooks.com



# Acknowledgments

This book was completed with the considerable help of my friends Tom Kailbourn, Tom Jett, Jim Gilmore, Dana Bell, and Sean Hert. The US Army Transportation, especially Alisha Hamel, Alexander Wick, and Vincent Falcon, went out of their way to be helpful. The resources of the National Archives, Army Aviation Museum, and San Diego Air & Space Museum provided many of the images. Those images without other credit are from Defense Visual Information Center. Neither this book nor any of the others could have been completed without the ongoing help and support of my darling wife, Denise.

# Contents

# Introduction

With tandem, contrarotating rotors swinging above an aluminum fuselage with round porthole windows, the lines of the CH-47 Chinook have become an icon of United States heavy-lift helicopters, owing in no small part to its sixty-year-plus service life—which some experts predict will ultimately reach a century of service.

While conventional helicopters require a torque-counteracting tail rotor, which consumes 15 percent of the engine power, tandem-rotor helicopters can put all the engine power into lift. The price for this increase in power is a substantially more complicated transmission and control system.

The US military has been interested in tandem-rotor helicopters since at least the 1947 XR-11 Dragonfly. However, it was engineer Frank N. Piasecki, then heading Piasecki Helicopter Corporation, who made the tandem-rotor helicopter viable for military use. Beginning with the PV-3 (HRP-2) Harp, popularly known as the "Flying Banana," Piasecki Helicopter Corporation supplied the military with an array of tandem-rotor helicopters, including the XHJP-1, later designated the HUP-1 Mule, and the H-21 "Shawnee." By 1957, the firm no longer employed Piasecki, who went on to found Piasecki Aircraft. When the H-21 arrived in Vietnam in December 1961, to become the first US tandem-rotor chopper to see combat, its manufacturer—now known as Vertol Aircraft Corporation—had begun work on a new, turbine-powered, tandem-rotor aircraft: the V-107.

The Vertol V-107 was born from a company-initiated study of what the US military would want in a twin-turbine helicopter. Thomas Pepper, chief of preliminary design for Vertol, spoke to a number of Army experts in air mobility and found that what the Army wanted was essentially a flying 2½-ton truck. The initial Army interview was followed by additional, detailed interviews with Marine, Navy, NACA, and Army personnel. The result of these interviews laid the framework of specifications for a rear-loading, easily maintainable, and easily retrofitted helicopter with high-mounted engines (protecting the engines from foreign objects, and ground personnel from exhaust and noise), suitable for carrier operations and permitting indiscriminate loading of personnel or cargo.

Vertol designers studied no fewer than 300 possible configurations before settling on what they dubbed their Model 107. On July 22, 1957, the company presented a three-step plan to the Army for the creation of the Model 107. This plan was in part conditioned on the Army loaning engines to Vertol for use in the prototype, then using the information gained from the construction and testing of the prototype toward development of a new medium-transport helicopter.

Rollout for the prototype was March 31, 1958, with the first flight lifting off from Philadelphia International Airport on April 22, 1958. The military designation for the Model 107 was the YHC-1. The contract initially called for the construction of ten YHC-1s, but after an initial review the Army felt that the Model 107 was too small for a transport aircraft, and too large for an assault helicopter. An enlarged version, Model 114, which will be discussed later, was designed and was designated the YHC-1B, and the model 107 became the YHC-1A. While the Army ardently pursued further development of the YHC-1B, the Navy and Marines opted for the smaller YHC-1A, which became the CH-46 Sea Knight.

Nearly a decade before the Boeing CH-47, Sikorsky introduced its H-34. Powered by a piston engine, the H-34 ably served the US Army, Navy, and Marines as a military heavy-lift helicopter from the mid-1950s through the Vietnam War. *National Archives*

First flying in 1952, the Piasecki H-21 was a tandem-rotor transport chopper used by the US Army and US Air Force. Dubbed the "Flying Banana" because of its shape, it was well suited to operations in extreme cold. The H-21 was the mainstay of the Army's heavy-lift helicopter operations until the advent of the CH-47 Chinook. *National Archives*

One of the first large helicopters, the Piasecki H-16 was nearly the size of a DC-4 transport and could carry forty-seven men. Only two of the H-16 tandem-rotor aircraft were built, with the first flight occurring on October 23, 1953. The program was canceled after the second prototype crashed on January 5, 1956, killing the two crewmen. *National Archives*

In the mid-1950s, Vertol Aircraft conducted a study of the American military's future needs for cargo helicopters. The concept of air mobility was coming to the fore in military thinking, and the Army desired a helicopter with the same carrying capabilities as a standard 2½-ton truck. On the basis of those findings, Vertol privately undertook the design and development of a medium-lift helicopter with tandem rotors, which had the company designation V-107. The twin General Electric YT58-GE-6 turbine engines were housed in the rear rotor pylon. The Army received three prototypes in 1957, designating them YHC-1A, one of which is seen here in a May 1960 photo, by which time Vertol had merged with Boeing and been renamed Boeing Vertol. *National Archives*

The Boeing Vertol YHC-1A had a tricycle landing gear, as seen in this frontal view at Fort Benning, Georgia, in May 1960. These prototypes were powered by General Electric YT58-GE-6 engines, and the fuselages were watertight, for landings on water. *National Archives*

The YHC-1A had a spacious interior, with folding seats for passengers. A man is seated in the forward right folding seat. There were an uninterrupted floor, sidewalls, and ceiling in the cargo compartment for the easy loading of men, vehicles, and cargo. *National Archives*

A rear ramp was a feature of the Boeing Vertol YHC-1A, to permit easy boarding and egress for troops, cargo, and vehicles. The two rotor pylons were tall, in order to cut down on the amount of dust the rotors churned up when on or near the ground. *National Archives*

The Boeing Vertol 107-II was a civilian and export version of the Model YHC-1A. An example is seen here in corporate livery, with square windows for the passengers, landing at the Pentagon's helipad. Its civil registration number was N6674D. *National Archives*

The first of the three Boeing Vertol YHC-1As was assigned US Army serial number 58-5514 and tail number 85514. In 1962, these prototypes were redesignated YCH-46C. They served as the basis for the CH-46 Sea Knight helicopters. *Army Aviation Museum*

# DEVELOPMENT

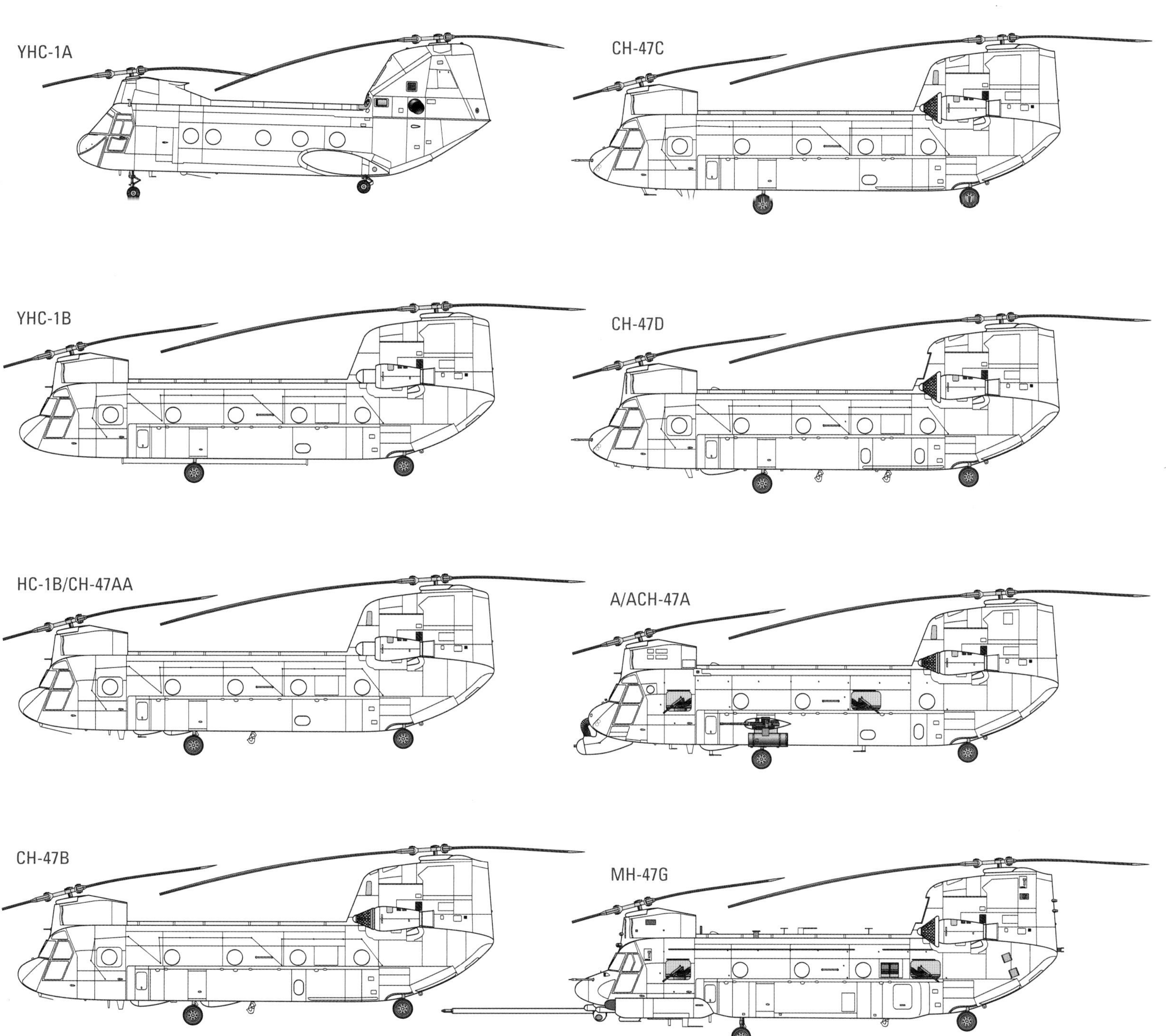

CHAPTER 1

# The Chinook through Vietnam

On June 25, 1958, the Army issued an invitation for a General Management Proposal for the US Army Medium Transport Helicopter program, which was intended to produce a replacement for the CH-21, CH-34, and CH-37.

Five firms—Bell, Kaman, McDonnell, Sikorsky, and Vertol—responded with proposals for what was known as Weapon System SS471L. Vertol offered several engine options, including a three-engine/four-rotor-blade Lycoming T55-L-3 (2,200 shaft horsepower [shp] each) configuration, a four-engine GE T64-GE-8 (2,810 shp each) scenario, or a two-engine GE T64-GE-2 (2,650 shp each) design. With the T55 configuration, the aircraft was expected to have four-bladed, 59-foot rotors, weigh a gross 33,703 pounds, and be capable of a maximum speed of 150 knots.

On March 4, 1959, the Joint Army / Air Force Source Selection Board recommended that Vertol be awarded the management contract for the medium-transport helicopter. Due to Army funding problems, the Air Force was asked to negotiate a development contract for the new aircraft (which Vertol designated the Model 114). The nineteen-million-dollar contract, awarded in June 1959, was for engineering, tooling, five airframes, a mockup, and initial testing of the Model 114, which bore the military designation YHC-1B.

Because of changes in the design gross weight, reset at 33,000 pounds, only two Lycoming T-55-L5 turboshaft engines rated at 1,940 shp each, turning two three-bladed rotors, were required. The overall fuselage length was established as 51 feet.

On November 16, 1959, Vertol and Boeing announced that Boeing was seeking to acquire Vertol, and on March 31, 1960, the deal was finalized and Vertol became a division of Boeing. Thus, since the YHC-1B first flew on September 21, 1961, it can be considered a Boeing product.

With some improvements and redesignated the CH-47A under the new US Tri-Service aircraft designation system, the Chinook helicopter went into production. It was powered by two Lycoming T55-L-7 engines, rated at 2,650 shp each. The Army designated the CH-47A as its official medium helicopter in October 1963, and a total of 349 were completed.

As helicopter-borne-infantry tactics were refined during the Vietnam War, the need for heavily armed and armored support helicopters became apparent. Seeking something heavier than the UH-1C Huey gunship, the Army turned to Boeing Vertol. On June 23, 1965, the company proposed creating the ACH-47A gunship. A contract was signed on June 30, 1965, and the next week work began on the first example, serial number 64-13145.

The aircraft first flew on November 6, 1965, and was delivered to the Army the next month. It was soon joined by three additional production ACH-47A aircraft.

Each ACH-47A carried five M60D 7.62 × 51 mm machine guns or M2HB .50-caliber machine guns and two M24A1 20 mm cannons mounted on stub wings, fed with 800 rounds of ammo. Also on the stub wings were shackles for holding two XM159B/XM159C nineteen-tube 2.75-inch rocket launchers or two M18/M18A1 7.62 × 51 mm gun pods. A single M75 40 mm grenade launcher was housed in an XM5 turret under the nose. Five hundred rounds of ammunition were supplied for the XM5.

Three of the four aircraft—64-13149, "Easy Money"; 64-13151, "Stump Jumper"; and 64-13154, "Birth Control"—deployed to Vung Tau, Vietnam, in June 1966, designated as the 53rd Aviation Detachment (Provisional), 1st Cavalry Division. "Co$t of Living," 64-13145, initially remained stateside. After "Stump Jumper" was lost in a taxi accident in August 1966, "Co$t of Living" went overseas as well. This ACH-47A shot itself down in May 1967, when a cannon

The Army decided that it required a larger medium-lift helicopter than the YHC-1A, so in May 1959 it ordered five YHC-1B service-test prototypes. These differed from the YHC-1A in that they had a longer fuselage, quadricycle rather than tricycle landing gear, and turbine engines in external pods rather than housed in the aft rotor pylon. In addition, the YHC-1B had a long sponson or pod on each side of the lower part of the fuselage that housed the fuel tanks, electronics equipment, and supports for the landing gear. Shown here is the fourth YHC-1B, registration number 59-4985. At the time, the rotors were not installed, but Vertol "touched in" the rotors when they sent this photo to the Army. The YHC-1B would prove to be the basis for the CH-47 Chinook helicopter. *National Archives*

Lacking its aft rotor, this Boeing Vertol YHC-1B, registration number 59-4985, is viewed from the right side. These service-test YHC-1Bs had a capacity of 10,100 pounds of internal cargo or 16,000 pounds of external cargo. For the purposes of external cargo, the helicopter was equipped with a winch-operated 16,000-pound cargo hook on the belly. Folding seats were included in the cargo compartment for thirty-three troops, compared with twenty-two passengers in the YHC-1A.

mounting pin failed, and all eight crew perished. "Birth Control" was shot down in February 1968, and while the crew of "Easy Money" rescued the personnel, the gunship was lost. Because tactics required that the aircraft operate in pairs, "Easy Money" was withdrawn from service and is today preserved in Alabama.

While the CH-47A was well received and successful, as is so often the case, there was a desire to increase performance. Toward this end, the first improved model was the CH-47B, which utilized T55-L-7C engines, each generating 2,850 shp and equipped with improved rotor blades with a steel main spar and honeycomb trailing edges, versus the CH-47A's aluminum main spar and fiberglass trailing edges. These and other improvements boosted the maximum gross weight of the CH-47B to 33,000 pounds, a 4,500-pound increase over the CH-47A.

Despite the improvements brought about by the introduction of the B model in 1967, that model remained in production for less than a year (May 10, 1967, through February 28, 1968) before being superseded by the CH-47C. The CH-47C, which first flew in experimental form on October 14, 1967, was the result of an effort to meet an Army requirement for increased range. To meet this requirement, engineers at Boeing Vertol, as Vertol had been renamed following the March 31, 1960, acquisition by the West Coast–based aviation behemoth, increased the fuel capacity from the 621 gallons of the CH-47B to 1,100 gallons. During ferry flights, this could be further augmented by adding four fuel bladders in the cargo compartment, increasing range to over 1,000 miles at 10,000 feet. This capability allowed the CH-47C to self-deploy to Europe, as was demonstrated in August 1979 by Operation Northern Leap, when Chinooks flew from Fort Carson, Colorado, to Heidelberg Army Air Field, Germany, with intermediate stops in Iowa, Pennsylvania, Maine, Canada, Greenland, Iceland, and England.

Later, both the CH-47B and the CH-47C were fitted with crash-resistant fuel tanks, which reduced their integral fuel capacities to 566 and 1,036 gallons, respectively. The transmission

YHC-1B, serial number 59-4985, appears with only the forward rotor head installed. The photo was taken to document the ability of the helicopter's ramp and cargo compartment to accommodate a truck as large as the Dodge M37 ¾-ton truck.

was upgraded, as well as in time the engines. While the CH-47C initially used the 2,850 shp T55-L-7C engine, after production of 106 examples (subsequently dubbed the "Baby C") the improved 3,750 shp T55-L-11 began to be installed. These aircraft were for a while referred to as the "Super C." In time the Baby C aircraft were upgraded to Super C configuration.

In addition to the increased fuel capacity, several other improvements were marked by the introduction of the CH-47C. Among these are larger dust and debris screens for engine air intake, an uprated driveshaft system, and dual automatic flight control and dual Stability Augmentation Systems vibration dampeners. During production, new rotor blades, developed with the aid of NASA, began to be installed. The new high-lift cambered blades were made of steel, aluminum, and fiberglass.

The CH-47C began arriving in Vietnam in September 1968. There, the additional capabilities were quickly appreciated, especially the ability to lift heavy loads (up to 10,000 pounds) in the high elevations of the Central Highlands, where previous Chinooks had been restricted to 7,000 pounds.

Production of the CH-47C totaled 288 units, with 224 of these being delivered during the Vietnam War. A total of 166 of the type were deployed in that conflict, where twenty-six were lost due to enemy action or accidents. One of those was 67-18529, shot down on February 16, 1973; three weeks *after* the Paris Peace Accords were signed. The only casualty of the crash, and the last Army Aviation member killed in action in Vietnam, was SP5 James L. Scroggins, previously awarded the Distinguished Flying Cross for saving his crew.

The second Boeing Vertol YHC-1B service-test helicopter, registration number 59-4983, shown during a test flight on October 19, 1961, was the first Chinook helicopter to fly, making its maiden flight on September 21, 1961, with Boeing Vertol test pilot Leonard La Vassar at the controls. The US Army accepted this helicopter on April 24, 1964, and it served until stricken from the rolls on March 1, 1970. *National Archives*

A Boeing Vertol YHC-1B, presumably serial number 59-4983, hovers feet above the ground in front of a hangar. A star-and-bars national insignia is on its belly. Parked on the hardstand in front of the hangar are several Boeing Vertol 107-II helicopters. *National Archives*

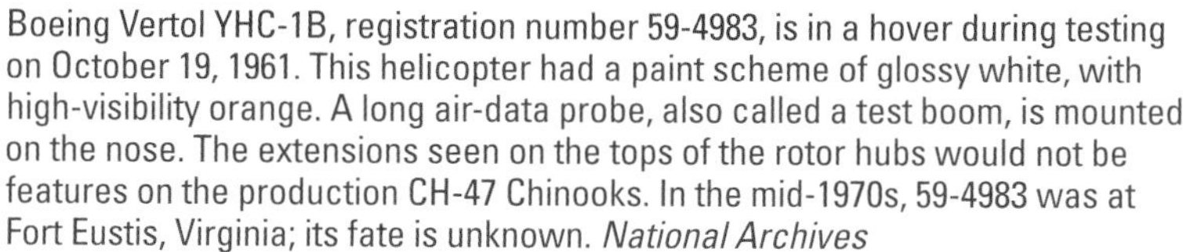

Boeing Vertol YHC-1B, registration number 59-4983, is in a hover during testing on October 19, 1961. This helicopter had a paint scheme of glossy white, with high-visibility orange. A long air-data probe, also called a test boom, is mounted on the nose. The extensions seen on the tops of the rotor hubs would not be features on the production CH-47 Chinooks. In the mid-1970s, 59-4983 was at Fort Eustis, Virginia; its fate is unknown. *National Archives*

The same helicopter shown in the two preceding photos, Boeing Vertol YHC-1B, serial number 59-4983, is viewed from the right side during tests on October 19, 1961. Escape hatches were outlined for rescue workers' ease of identification. *National Archives*

YHC-1B, serial number 59-4985, was used for a variety of test purposes. Here, it is conducting a sling test at Aberdeen Proving Ground, Maryland, in October 1966, to assess the helicopter's ability to transport the lightweight launcher of the Lance Missile System. *National Archives*

The third prototype YHC-1B, serial number 59-4984, is preserved at the US Army Transportation Museum at Fort Eustis, Newport News, Virginia. It served as a test aircraft and later was sent to Fort Eustis to serve as a maintenance trainer. After spending several decades in outdoor storage, the Chinook was restored by Summit Aviation, in Delaware; since 2014, it has been displayed at Fort Eustis. *Tom Jett*

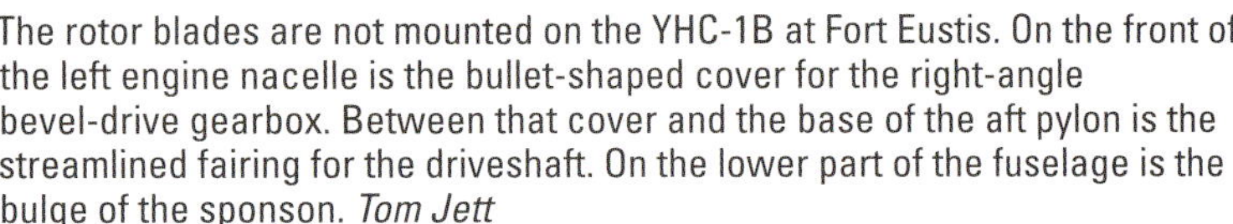

The rotor blades are not mounted on the YHC-1B at Fort Eustis. On the front of the left engine nacelle is the bullet-shaped cover for the right-angle bevel-drive gearbox. Between that cover and the base of the aft pylon is the streamlined fairing for the driveshaft. On the lower part of the fuselage is the bulge of the sponson. *Tom Jett*

The ramp is viewed from the left rear, with the left auxiliary loading ramp, which is hinged to the main ramp, to the lower right. Also in view is the left rear landing gear, with its single wheel and tire. *Tom Jett*

The rear of the wall of the left side of the aft fuselage of the third prototype YHC-1B is viewed from above the ramp. Lightening holes are prevalent in the frame members. *Tom Jett*

The left rear landing gear is viewed from the outboard side, its wheels secured with chocks. Also in view is the left side of the lowered ramp. *Tom Jett*

A view of the left rear landing gear, taken from the right rear, above the ramp, shows the system of struts and drag links that supported the wheel. Running along the lower strut is the hydraulic line for the disk brake; the brake is located to the rear of the axle. *Tom Jett*

Nestled in the upper rear of the aft fuselage, above the ramp opening, is the auxiliary power unit, which supplied all the necessary electrical and hydraulic power to operate the helicopter on the ground. This appears to be a later type of APU, as installed in CH-47Ds. The exhaust projects from the rear of the fuselage, toward the left. *Tom Jett*

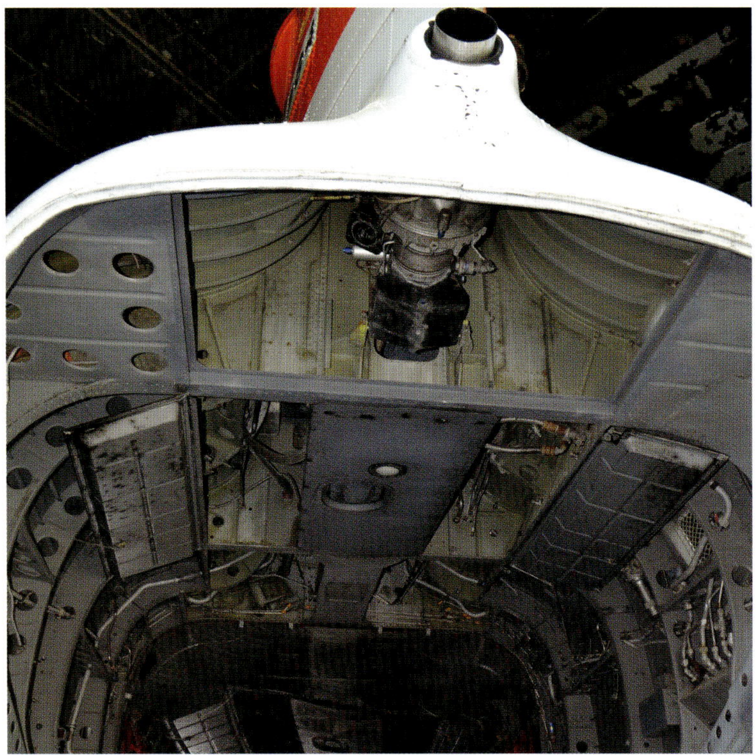

The ceiling of the aft fuselage is viewed from above the ramp, showing the APU and its exhaust in the foreground. Quilted soundproofing material is on the ceiling in the background. *Tom Jett*

Details of the right side of the interior of the aft fuselage above the ramp, including the networks of hydraulic lines, are displayed. Part of the right rear landing gear is in view. *Tom Jett*

The cabin, the part of the fuselage between the cockpit (*background*) and the aft fuselage, is viewed from the aft end. The crew seat bottoms to the right are secured in the raised position, showing their tubular metal frames, while those to the left are lowered. Quilted soundproofing panels are installed. *Tom Jett*

The raised seat bottoms on the left side of the cabin are viewed facing aft. Below the seats is a long heat and ventilation duct. *Tom Jett*

The cabin of the third prototype YHC-1B is viewed from the forward end, facing aft, showing details of the soundproofing and the personnel seats. Several storage pouches are attached with Velcro to the soundproofing, including one for litter straps. *Tom Jett*

On the left side of the forward end of the cabin is an emergency exit panel with a round window. The soundproof panels on the forward bulkhead of the compartment have access panels for the avionics compartment, *left*, and the heater, *right*. To the right is the cabin door, which consists of two sections: an upper one with a round window, which has been raised up on its tracks, and a hinged lower one, which forms a step when open. The forward bracket for that section is visible at the lower right. *Tom Jett*

The upper section of the door is in its raised position, with a roller assembly on each corner of the door resting in the tracks. On the center bottom of the door section are the lock handle and the lock-actuating links. *Tom Jett*

The forward left corner of the cabin is seen, including the left personnel seats, the emergency exit panel, and the door to the cockpit. *Tom Jett*

On the left side of the passageway from the cabin to the cockpit is a bay containing the control system for interconnecting the cockpit controls with the power plants and the rotor system. *Tom Jett*

The cockpit is partially visible from the passageway from the cabin. The copilot's seat is to the left, and the pilot's is to the right. Above the console between the seats is the center instrument panel, to the sides of which are the copilot's and the pilot's instrument panels. *Tom Jett*

The copilot's seat, shoulder harness, and safety belt, as well as the left side of the cockpit, are depicted. The small lever with a round knob on the side of the seat, to the front of the safety belt, is the control for adjusting the height of the seat; below it is the lever for adjusting the seat horizontally. *Tom Jett*

As seen from the passageway to the rear of the cockpit, mounted at an angle above the center of the windshield is the overhead switch and circuit-breaker panel. *Tom Jett*

The cockpit instrument panel is lacking some of its gauges and controls; where such features are absent, placards replicating them are affixed to the panel. To the fronts of the seats are the pilot's and copilot's cyclic sticks. *Tom Jett*

On the center console to the lower left is the engine-condition panel, with levers and stops for flight, ground, and stop settings. To the right of that panel, on the right side of the console, is the pilot's collective grip. *Tom Jett*

The copilot's station is illustrated, with his collective grip visible to the left of his seat, and his cyclic stick, also known as the pitch-roll control, to the front of the seat. The yellow panel with diagonal black stripes on the top of the center instrument panel contains the fire-extinguisher agent switch and the fire-detector test switch. *Tom Jett*

The grip of the copilot's cyclic control is viewed from the right. The round device at the top of the grip is the stick trim switch. On the copilot's instrument panel are several real gauges and a number of facsimile gauges. *Tom Jett*

Below the copilot's instrument panel are his footrests and directional pedals. The grip of the cyclic control is at the upper center. *Tom Jett*

In a view of the grip of the pilot's cyclic control from the left, at the top is the stick trim switch; the red button adjacent to that switch is the centering-device release. The red button on the center of the grip is for triggering the flare dispenser, and near the bottom of the grip is the cargo hook release. *Tom Jett*

At the center is the pilot's collective grip. On the box on its front end, rpm adjustment switches are on the left, the searchlight control is on its center, and on the right is the searchlight filament (SL FIL) control. *Tom Jett*

A view of the rear of the right side of the fuselage of the third prototype YHC-1B includes the engine nacelle, with the bullet-shaped cover for the right-angle bevel-drive gearbox on the front and the stainless-steel exhaust nozzle on the rear. The dark shape on the underside of the nacelle is a vent. Running up the side of the fuselage at the center are recessed maintenance steps with sprung covers. *Tom Jett*

The aft pylon, the cover for the right-angle bevel-drive gearbox, the driveshaft fairing, and the right engine nacelle are observed from the front. The black stripes above the maintenance steps help crewmen locate where the steps are. *Tom Jett*

The middle and forward parts of the right side of the fuselage and sponson of the third prototype YHC-1B are observed. In the background is the right forward-landing gear, which is equipped with two wheels. *Tom Jett*

The forward right (*foreground*) and left (*background*) landing gear are in view. On the sponson above the right landing gear is a position light with a green, teardrop-shaped lens. *Tom Jett*

The upper and lower panels of the cabin door are open, on the right side of the fuselage just aft of the cockpit. Details of the two brackets upon which the lower panel swivels are evident. To the lower rear of the pilot's door is the jettison handle for that door. *Tom Jett*

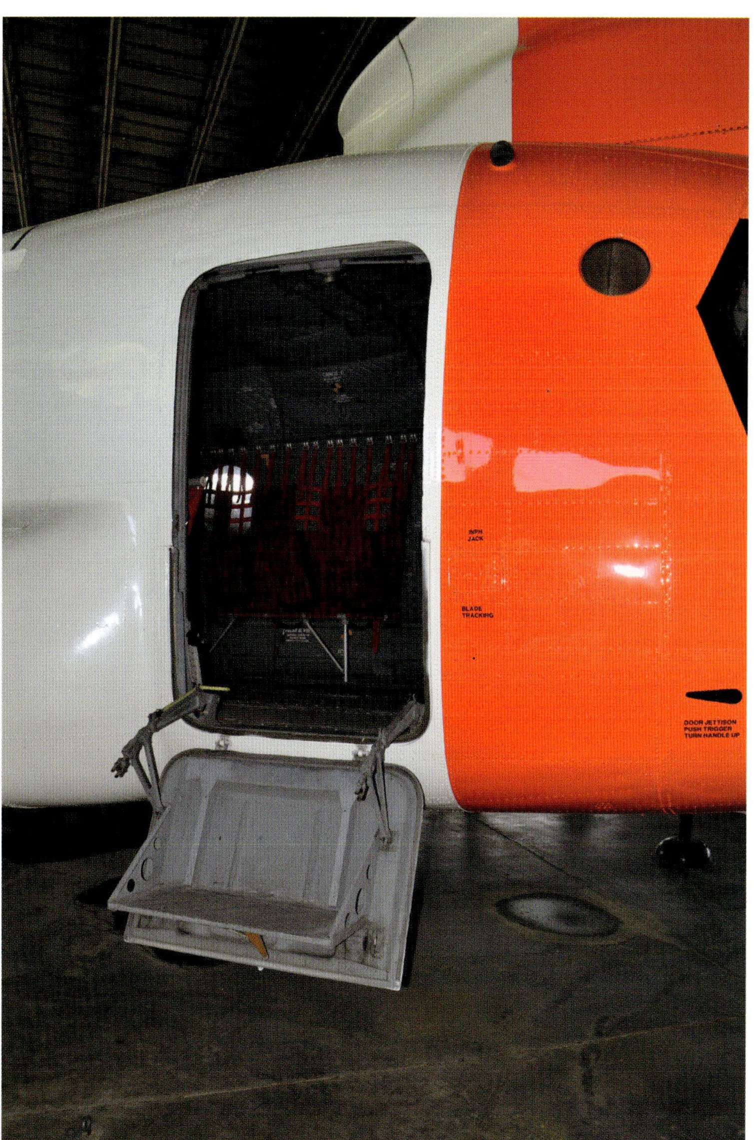


The lower panel of the cabin door incorporates a boarding step, with a triangular support with three lightening holes on each side. *Tom Jett*

The entire right side of the third prototype YHC-1B is seen from the front of the aircraft. The dark, round feature to the rear of the upper part of the pilot's door is the air intake for the heater, above and slightly aft of which is the exhaust pipe for the heater. *Tom Jett*

The YHC-1B is observed from the front, showing the windshield, the chin windows, and the forward pylon. Each side of the windshield is supplied with a wiper, mounted above the windshield. The two disc-shaped objects on each of the chin windows are yaw-sensing ports, which transmit information on sideslip to the stability augmentation system. *Tom Jett*

The CH-47A was the first full-scale production model of the Chinook. It was powered by two Lycoming T55-L-7 engines, rated at 2,650 shp each. Delivery of this model began in August 1962, and the type was standardized in October of the following year. The third production CH-47A, serial number 60-3450, was the first one to be delivered to the US Army and is seen here during a static-line paratrooper jump exercise. *National Archives*

The fourth CH-47A Chinook, serial number 60-3451, is parked in a field while assisting to transport a missile battery. A large part of the Chinook's mission as envisioned by the Army was the rapid movement of artillery from one emplacement to another. *Army Aviation Museum*

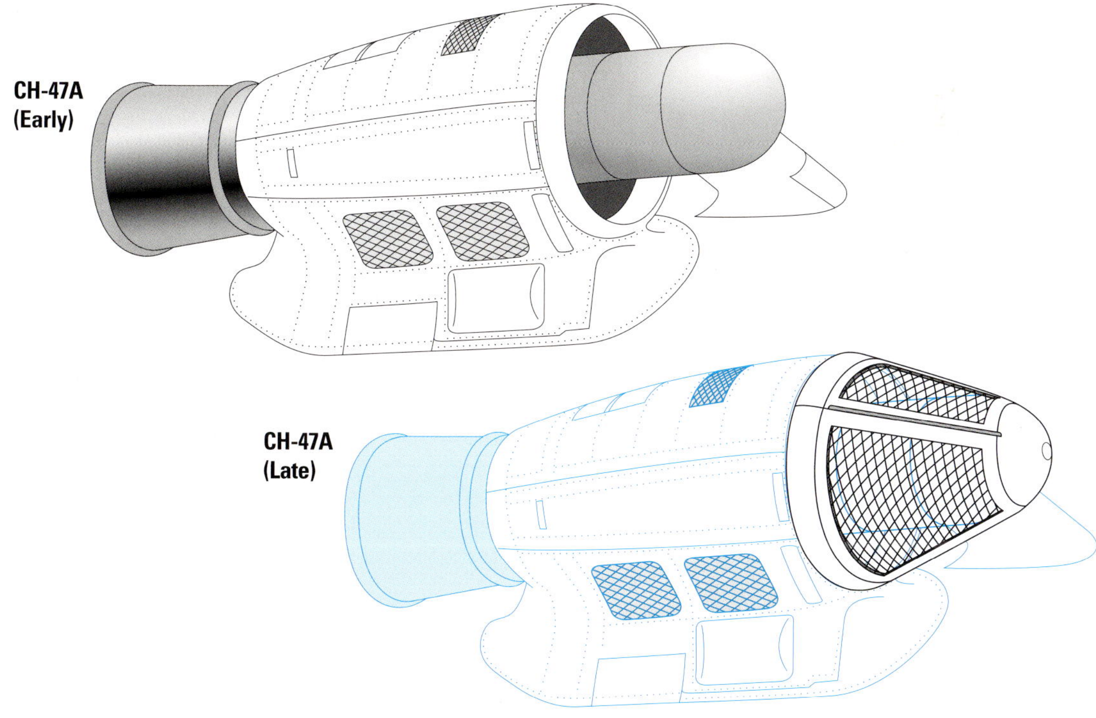


The engine pods of early- and late-production CH-47A Chinooks are compared in these diagrams. The late-production CH-47As had a conical screen over the engine intake to keep out foreign objects. The screen did not diminish engine performance.

Rotors folded for storage, a US Army CH-47A Chinook medium helicopter is viewed close-up from the front left at Fort Sill, Oklahoma, in October 1966. On the nose adjacent to the pilot's and copilot's lower windows are communications antennas. A panel marked "ACCESS" is between the antennas. On the sides of the fuselage were short mounting posts, called "standoffs," on which high-frequency wire antennas could be affixed. *National Archives*

CH-47A 66-0066 at Fort Sill, Oklahoma, in October 1966. Jutting below the chin of the helicopter, and also visible in the preceding photo, is a rearview mirror, with which the pilot and copilot could observe the operation of the cargo hook. This mirror later was omitted when the crew chief was tasked with monitoring the cargo hook. Toward the front of the fuselage pod is the open access hatch for the electronics compartment. *National Archives*

A tow tractor is hitched to the rear of CH-47 66-0066 at Fort Sill on October 17, 1966. The front landing gear had dual wheels, while the rear gears had single wheels. On top of the fuselage is a framework made of pipes, to support the folded rotor blades. *National Archives*

On the basis of early experience of helicopter operations in Vietnam, the Army Materiel Command, Aberdeen, Maryland, proposed an armed and armored version of the CH-47, capable of suppressing enemy fire and defeating small-arms fire at landing zones. This helicopter was designated ACH-47A, and Boeing Vertol converted four CH-47As to these gunships in late 1965. Two of them are shown here, showing their XM5 chin turrets with M75 40 mm grenade launcher and right stub wing with an M24A1 20 mm cannon and rocket pod. *Army Aviation Museum*

The ACH-47A had window-mounted .50-caliber machine guns. An ammunition feed chute connects from the nose to the 40 mm grenade-launcher turret. On the stub wing are an XM159 nineteen-round, 2.75-inch rocket-launcher pod and an M24A1 20 mm cannon. *Army Aviation Museum*

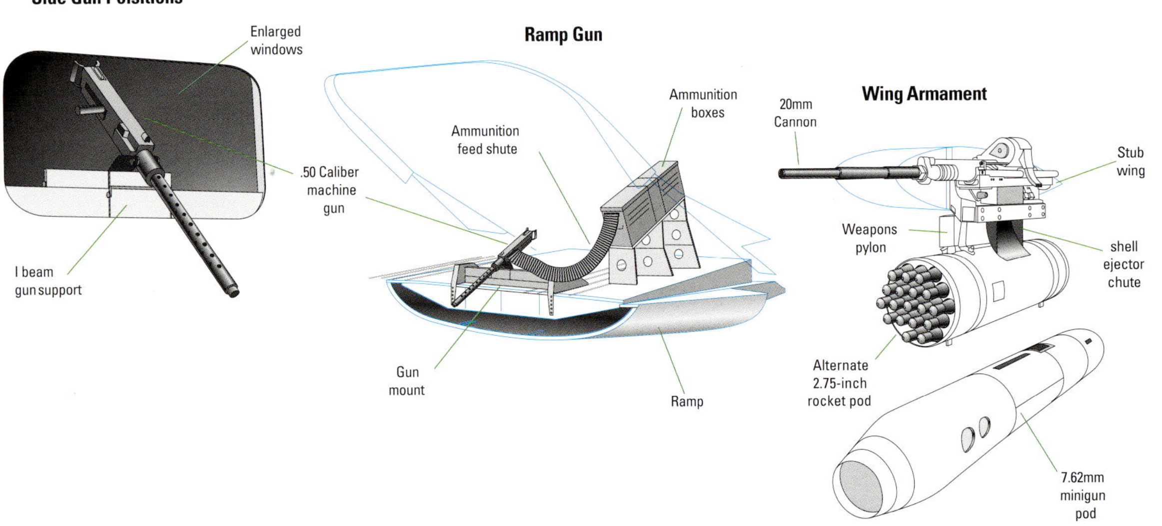


These diagrams show the weapons installed in the ACH-47A, including window-mounted .50-caliber machine guns, installation of a .50-caliber machine gun and ammunition box on the lowered ramp, and the choice of weapons carried on the stub wings.

An XM159 2.75-inch rocket pod is viewed close-up without the nineteen rockets loaded. The pods were mounted on pylons attached to the stub wings. A close view of the M24A1 20 mm cannon also is included, along with its ammo feed and cartridge-ejector chute. *Army Aviation Museum*

Col. John Harland Swenson, US Army, stands next to an ACH-47A, with armament on the right stub wing consisting of an M24A1 20 mm cannon over a General Electric M18E1 7.62 mm minigun, a pod-contained rotary gun, and 1,500 rounds of ammunition. *Army Aviation Museum*

One of the ACH-47As is seen from the left side during a hover. Light-colored horizontal bars are aft of the machine-gun windows, while a large, vertical bar is on the aft rotor pylon. The prominent chin turret made the ACH-47As unmistakable in profile. *Army Aviation Museum*

In collaboration with the US Army, Boeing Vertol commenced work on an experimental helicopter based on the CH-47 in January 1969. Designated the Model 347, this helicopter had a longer fuselage than the CH-47, in addition to having four-bladed rotors and a 45-foot wing. For this project, the Army bailed to Boeing Vertol a CH-47A, registration number 65-7992. The Model 347 made its first flight on May 27, 1970. *San Diego Air & Space Museum*

During the initial tests of the Boeing Vertol Model 347, the helicopter was fitted with fairings in the shoulder position, where the wings later would be mounted. The 347 was equipped with retractable landing gear. When retracted, the aft wheels remained exposed below the rear of the fuselage pylons, as seen in this photo of the helicopter in a low-level hover. Improvements to control noise and vibrations were incorporated in the Model 347. *Army Aviation Museum*

The extended fuselage of the Boeing Vertol Model 347 is apparent in this photo from the left side. This wings, installed after the initial flight tests, acted to unload the rotors and had variable incidence and full-span flaps. The one-off Model 347 (also called the BV-347) was conceived to develop and test concepts and components for future heavy-lift helicopters. The fuselage was 9 feet, 2 inches longer than that of the CH-47. *Army Aviation Museum*

Following the Model 347 test program, that one-off aircraft, registration number 65-7992, was used for the testing of an advanced fly-by-wire flight-control system for a heavy-lift helicopter. "HLH FLY BY WIRE" was marked high up on the fuselage aft of the cockpit. *National Archives*

The fly-by-wire control system replaced the traditional hydromechanical connections from the flight controls to the rotors with electrical connections. A retractable gondola on the belly of the HLH Fly by Wire served as a control station for external loads. *National Archives*

The HLH Fly by Wire has a cargo container handler slung underneath during tests at Davison Army Airfield, Virginia, in 1974. The rack-like container handler was designed to automatically lock on to the top of a cargo container, enabling rapid pickup and departure from the pickup site. This helicopter featured an automatic external load recovery system, enabling automated hover and cargo pickup. *National Archives*

The fixture called the cargo container handler has locked on to a cargo container in this photo taken at Davison Army Airfield in 1974, and the HLH Fly by Wire aircraft has lifted the container. The rearward-facing operator in the gondola controlled the helicopter during lifting operations by using a four-axis sidearm controller. Two lifting hooks were used, for better load stability, which also resulted in better flight stability. *National Archives*

In a final photo of the HLH Fly by Wire aircraft conducting heavy-lifting tests at Davison Army Airfield in 1974, the load operator is positioned in the gondola; he is wearing a helmet and is looking down toward the photographer. The gondola had clear panels on the sides and the floor, for better operator visibility. To the lower right is a cargo container with a container handler attached to it. *National Archives*

The CH-47B was an improved version of the CH-47B, with a stronger airframe and a higher-powered engine, for better performance in the heat of Southeast Asia. This version was powered by two Lycoming T55-L-7C turbine engines rated at 2,850 shp. Two key visual identifying features of the CH-47B compared with the A model were a flat, rather than sharp, trailing edge for the aft rotor pylon, and strakes on the bottom rear of each fuselage sponson and on each side of the lower part of the ramp. Shown here is CH-47B, serial number 67-18439, showing the ease with which it could lift a truck during a demonstration tour in Europe in 1967. *San Diego Air & Space Museum*

A CH-47B performs a low, downward-tilted hover maneuver over an airfield during a 1967 demonstration tour in Europe. The left sponson strake may be seen from a point below the next-to-rear round window, to the rear of the sponson. *San Diego Air & Space Museum*

Civilian and military spectators are on hand to watch a demonstration of a CH-47B at an air base in Europe in 1967. The CH-47B was faster and had greater range than the CH-47A and was able to lift heavier loads to greater altitudes in warm climates. *San Diego Air & Space Museum*

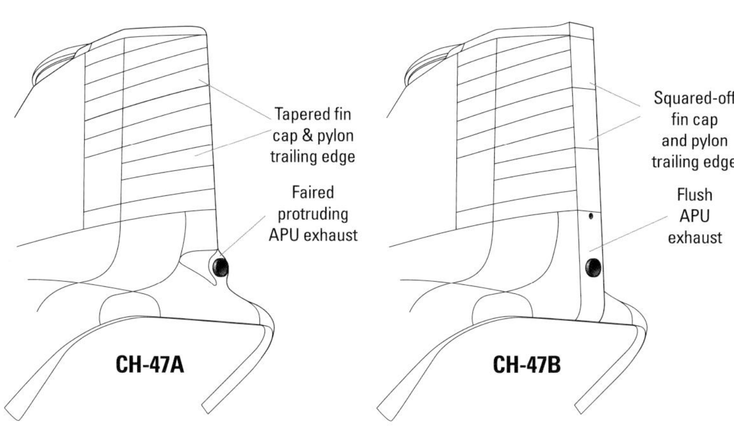


The aft rotor pylon of the CH-47A had a rounded top rear corner and a sharp trailing edge, while the aft rotor pylon of the CH-47B had a rounded upper rear corner and a flattened trailing edge. Differences in the APU exhausts also are illustrated.

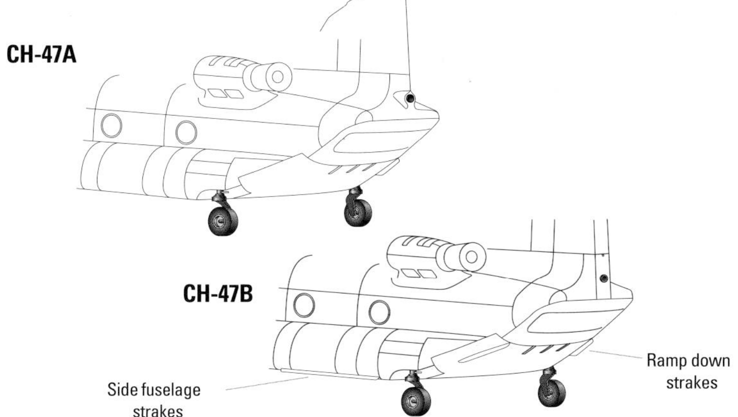


For the CH-47B, and continuing in subsequent models of the Chinook, a strake was added toward the rear of each fuselage sponson and on each side of the lower part of the ramp, for better longitudinal stability during ramp-down flight operations.

The CH-47C was the result of an Army requirement for a helicopter that could transport a slung load of 15,000 pounds a distance of 30 nautical miles at 4,000 feet and in temperatures up to 95 degrees Fahrenheit. These requirements were satisfied with the help of two Lycoming T55-L-11C turboshaft engines rated at 3,750 shp each, coupled to 6,000 shp transmissions. In addition, the airframe was further strengthened, the pitot tube on the front of the forward rotor pylon was deleted, and two new pitot tubes on extension posts were mounted on the nose. *National Archives*

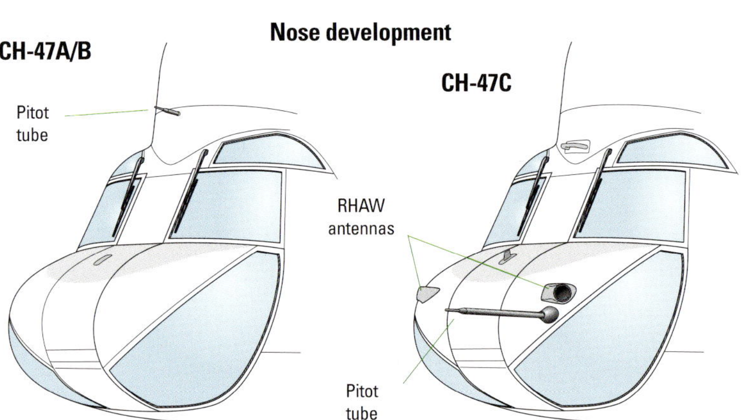


The pitot tube on the front of the forward rotor pylon on the CH-47Bs was replaced on the CH-47Cs by a glide-slope antenna in that position, and a new pitot tube and two radar homing and warning (RHAW) antennas now were installed on the nose.

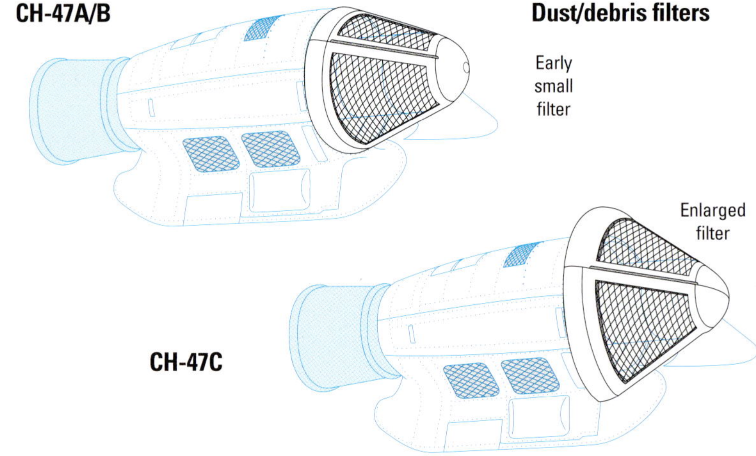


The dust and debris filters installed on CH-47Bs and retrofitted on some CH-47As were enlarged for the CH-47C, with the rear of the filter having a larger diameter than that of the engine intake. This allowed for bypass air to exit the filter.

CHAPTER 2

# CH-47D: The Post-Vietnam Workhorse

Much of the Army's inventory of Chinooks saw heavy use in Vietnam, with 577 aircraft, or 85 percent of the Chinooks built prior to 1973, having been involved in the conflict. Of those, 141 were lost to accidents or enemy action, and those that survived showed obvious signs of heavy use. That use, while proving the soundness of the basic design, also pointed to some areas that were worthy of improvement.

A complete rebuild and modernization plan was devised, which would involve stripping the airframe, repairing and renewing the airframe structure as needed, and then installing numerous improved components. So extensive was this work and modification that the resultant aircraft was given a new model number—the CH-47D—and aircraft subjected to this process were given new serial numbers as well. The result truly was a new helicopter—not merely a rebuilt one—and thus the new serial numbers.

All existing CH-47 models, A, B, or C, could be put through this process. In fact, the three prototypes for the CH-47D program were originally of different model numbers. The first aircraft, 65-08008, was a CH-47A, while 67-18479 was a CH-47B, and 67-18538 represented the CH-47C.

Among the biggest improvements found in the D model were increased redundancy in the electrical and hydraulic systems. The CH-47Ds would feature improved engines in the form of Lycoming T55-L-712 turbines, developing 4,075 shp each at takeoff. Through gearboxes, these turned fiberglass blades with a 32-inch cord (8 inches more than on the CH-47C), providing greater lift. New, armored crew seats were added, as were AN/APR-39V radar-warning and AN/ALQ-156 missile detection equipment. The fuel system was improved and made crash resistant, and armor protection was added for the transmission and oil coolers. For protection against shoulder-fired missiles, a M130 flare dispenser was added to the port side.

With the improvements, the CH-47D has a maximum gross weight of 50,000 pounds and can transport forty-four combat-ready troops. A multiple-hook external cargo system allows transport of sling loads of up to 28,000 pounds at speeds up to 115 miles per hour. The triple-hook system also allows the CH-47D to transport loads to multiple destinations simultaneously. The intention of the program was that the CH-47D would add about twenty years to the airframe life. As of 2014, forty-two US CH-47Ds had been lost in accidents, and seven were lost in combat, two were sold to Australia, and six were supplied to Canada, one of which was lost due to enemy action in Afghanistan.

The initial CH-47D prototype first flew on May 14, 1979. Preparations began at Boeing's Pennsylvania facility for series production the next year, with the first production D model making its maiden flight on February 26, 1982. The initial production aircraft were delivered to the 159th Assault Helicopter Battalion, 101st Airborne Division, Fort Campbell, Kentucky, on February 28, 1983.

The CH-47D program reprocessed 441 Chinooks, including 164 CH-47A, 75 CH-47B, and 200 CH-47C aircraft. This included eleven CH-47Cs that had been built for Iran by Augusta and seven from Australia. One aircraft, serial number 84-24166, crashed during a Boeing test flight and was not delivered to the Army. Two new CH-47Ds were built from the ground up (serial numbers 92-00367 and 92-00368), and a third new build, 98-02000, was put together from leftover bits and pieces at the Boeing plant and was fittingly dubbed "Mr. Potato Head."

The CH-47D was intended as a Chinook with greater reliability, better maintainability, and more power than previous models. The program included new-construction CH-47Ds as well as earlier-model Chinooks upgraded to CH-47D specifications. In this undated photograph, a CH-47D, serving as a test aircraft, is airlifting an M198 155 mm howitzer, weighing approximately 15,800 pounds. *National Archives*

Among the improvements included in the CH-47D were two Lycoming T55-L-712 turbine engines, three cargo hooks, a large opening in the front of the aft rotor pylon for oil-cooler ventilation, and two pitot tubes on the nose. In addition, the rotor blades, now fabricated from fiberglass, had a 32-inch chord, compared with 24 inches on the CH-47C. *Army Aviation Museum*

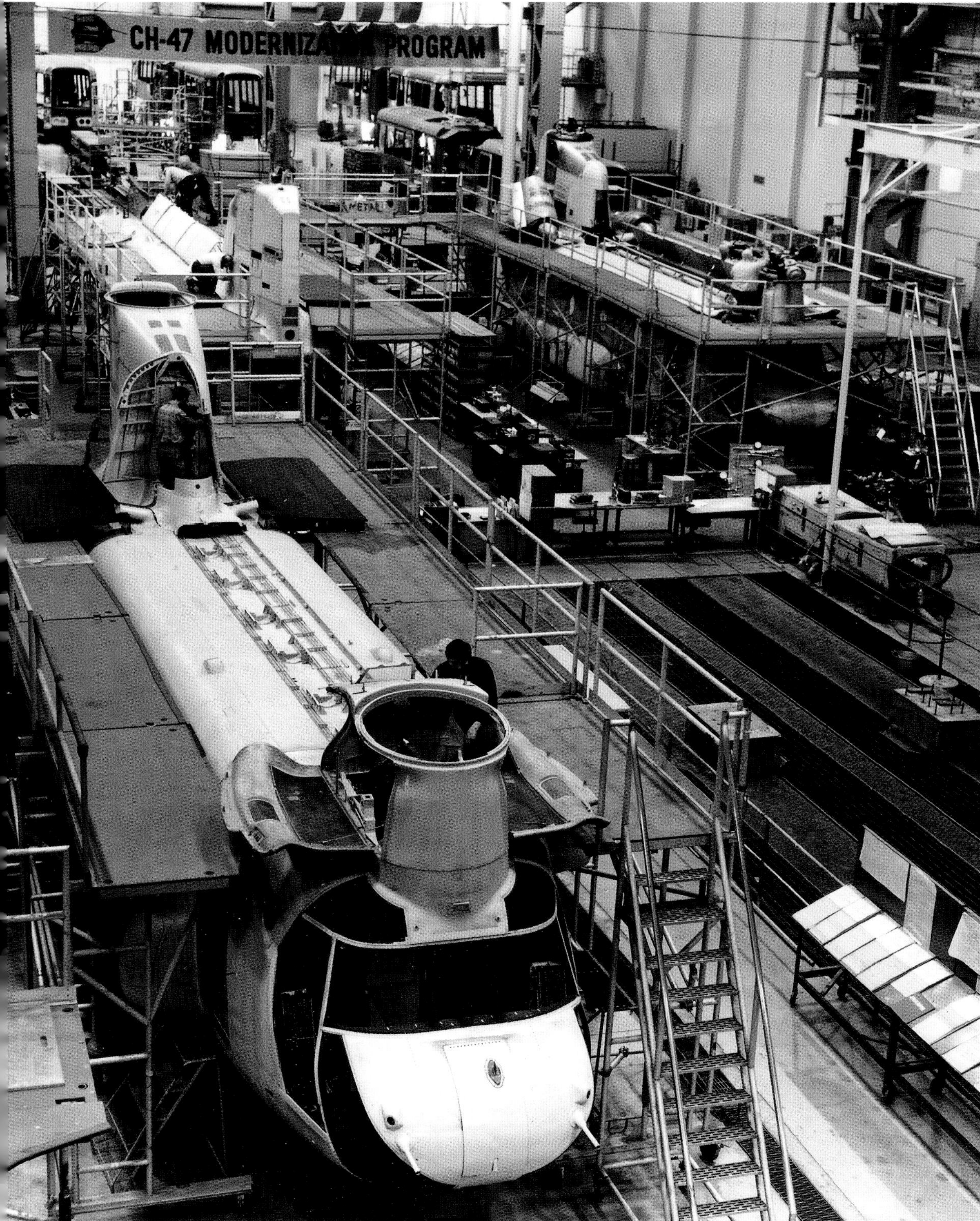


CH-47D airframes are under construction. Visible on the one in the foreground are the pitot-tube posts on the nose, the stressed-metal access doors that doubled as work platforms on the front pylon, and the channel for the main transmission driveshaft and various lines, which will receive a hinged cover along the length of the fuselage spine. The external engines and drivetrain made for fewer obstructions in the cargo compartment. *Army Aviation Museum*

On the fuselage just forward of the ramp opening on this CH-47D is an AN/ALE-29A flare dispenser. Details of the stainless-steel engine exhaust and the foreign-object screen on the front of the engine nacelle are shown. On the forward part of the fuselage is a high-frequency "towel bar" radio antenna. *Author*

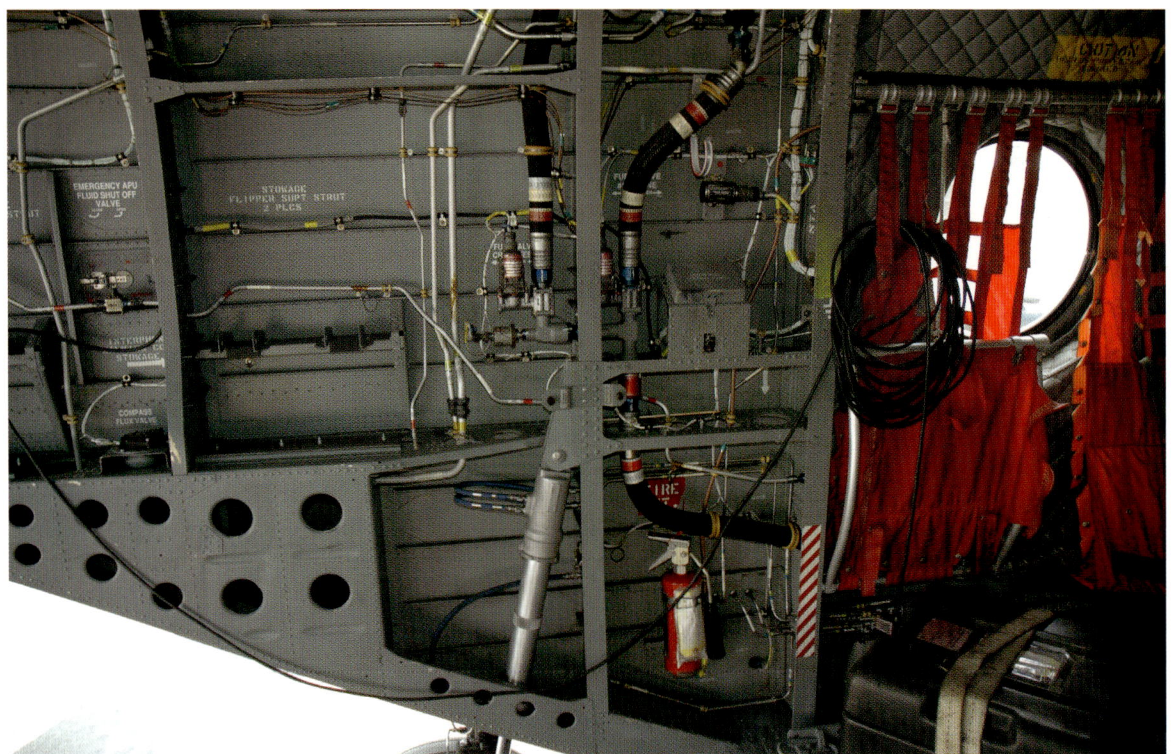


The left wall of the fuselage above the ramp of the CH-47D includes a maze of hydraulic, fuel, and electrical lines, with white stencils indicating various features. At the lower center are a fire extinguisher and the left ramp actuating cylinder. *Author*

This photo is a continuation of the preceding one, showing the upper right sector of the fuselage above the ramp. The light-colored box is the auxiliary power unit (APU) control box. *Author*

As seen in a view of the rear of the right side of the fuselage, much equipment and plumbing had been added to this area since the early Chinook helicopters. At the upper center is a maintenance panel for the hydraulic system and the transmission. Toward the right is the operating lever for the emergency hydraulic pump, for manually generating pressure for the utility hydraulic system. *Author*

On the upper part of the right sidewall of the cabin is the winch operator's station, featuring a recessed pan containing the hoist-control panel and a handgrip and cable containing the winch controls. *Author*

In a bay to the right front of the cabin is the heater, a 200,000 BTU/hour, combustion-type unit equipped with a blower, ducting, and regulating controls. Heat outlets are provided in the cockpit, and heating ducts run along the lengths of the lower parts of the sidewalls of the cabin. *Author*

The instrument panels in the cockpit of the CH-47D feature analog gauges. To the left is the copilot's instrument panel; to the right is the pilot's. Between those panels is the center instrument panel, which, in the CH-47 manuals, is considered part of the center console, which extends to between the seats. *Author*

A copilot's-eye view incorporates his instrument panel, cyclic control, directional pedals, and, *at lower left*, collective grip. The parameter of the downward visibility to the front and sides is evident. *Author*

The pilot's collective grip, to the left of his seat, the cyclic control stick and grip, and parts of the instrument panel are in view. *Author*

CHAPTER 3

# CH-47F: Twenty-First-Century Chinook

As the twentieth century ended, the Chinook was again upgraded. The latest model, the CH-47F, would incorporate advanced avionics. In the cockpit, the analog dials of the earlier Chinooks gave way to the Common Avionics Architecture System (CAAS), featuring five multifunction displays (MFD) replacing the old analog instruments. Another major avionics upgrade is the Digital Advanced Flight Control System (DAFCS), which provides unprecedented automatic hover control.

The structure of the aircraft was improved as well, with larger, but fewer, components, resulting in less vibration and inherently less maintenance. Powering the CH-47F, like all Chinooks, are a pair of Honeywell T55 turbine engines. However, the twenty-first-century CH-47 has a pair of Honeywell T55-L-714A engines developing 4,868 shp, more than twice the output of the T55s in the original YHC-1B.

The first three Engineering and Manufacturing Development (EMD) CH-47Fs, serial numbers 98-00011, 98-00012, and 03-08003, were remanufactured from CH-47D models, serial numbers 83-24107, 83-24115, and 83-24121. The first flight of the CH-47F model was in 2001. The rollout of the first production CH-47F was on June 15, 2006, and the first flight was on October 23, 2006.

While about half of the CH-47Fs produced have been built new from the ground up, the balance of the production was accomplished by removing certain key components from existing CH-47D aircraft and incorporating those components into the new airframe. Given that the CH-47Ds were themselves the result of an upgrade program, the result of this is that some aircraft have had multiple lives, such as CH-47A, 63-07906: it was delivered in June 1964, served in Vietnam, was converted into CH-47D 87-00096 in 1988, was deployed to Afghanistan, and then in 2012 became CH-47F 13-08109.

In October 2021, the Army awarded Boeing a $136 million contract to manufacture the first four CH-47F "Block II" production aircraft. Block 2 aircraft feature an even more powerful version of the T55 turbine, featuring "drop-in" capability to speed service, as well as improvements in the rotor drive, fuel system, and wiring. The resultant aircraft will boost the Chinook's weight to 54,000 pounds. Initially, the aircraft was to have a new style of rotor blade, yielding a 1,500-pound increase in lift. However, testing showed that the new swept-rotor-tip blades induced vibrations, which were a concern to the Army. The first four aircraft are expected to be delivered in late 2023 or early 2024.

The CH-47F is an improved version of the CH-47D, featuring upgraded Honeywell T55 engines rated at 4,868 shp; a revised airframe with easier inspection, maintenance, and repairs as well as less vibration and a longer service life; and improved avionics. The CH-47F first flew in 2001, and deliveries began in November 2006, with serial number 04-08071. Here, members of Bravo Company, 1st Battalion, 214th Aviation Regiment (General Support), are conducting phase maintenance on a CH-47F at Katterbach Army Airfield, Germany, on November 30, 2016. *DVIDS*

This CH-47F, serial number 13-08432, is undergoing phase maintenance in a hangar of Bravo Company, 1st Battalion, 214th Aviation Regiment (General Support), at Katterbach Army Airfield, Germany, on November 30, 2016. *DVIDS*

A CH-47F Chinook helicopter equipped with skis on the landing gear flies over a landing zone, having just dropped off paratroopers of a joint US Army–Japan Ground Self-Defense Force team during Exercise Arctic Aurora in Alaska on June 9, 2016. *DVIDS*

A CH-47F from the 12th Combat Aviation Brigade is preparing to airlift by sling an M777 155 mm howitzer from Archer Battery, Field Artillery Squadron, 2nd Cavalry Regiment, during an exercise at Grafenwoehr Training Area Germany, March 21, 2016. *DVIDS*

The crew chief of a Colorado Army National Guard CH-47F, registration number 09-08824, checks the sound of the engines before takeoff at the Army Aviation Support Facility, Buckley Air Force Base, Colorado, on March 3, 2016. *DVIDS*

A US Army CH-47F Chinook from 5th Battalion, 159th Aviation Regiment, based at Fort Eustis, Virginia, taxis at Hurlburt Field, Florida, on May 7, 2016, during Exercise Emerald Warrior 16, a US Special Operations Command readiness exercise. *DVIDS*

CHAPTER 4

# MH-47: The Special-Ops Taxi

Aircraft of the MH-47 family are specifically equipped for use by special-operations, heavy-assault helicopter companies. These Chinooks are among the variety of specialized helicopters operated by the 160th Special Operations Aviation Regiment (Airborne)—SOAR(A), based at Fort Campbell, Kentucky.

Three models of the MH-47 have been fielded since the first of the type, the MH-47D, was introduced in the mid-1980s. The twelve MH-47Ds were converted from existing aircraft through the addition of nose radar, an infrared camera, satellite communications, electronic countermeasures, improved navigational systems, and, most externally visible, an in-flight refueling probe and all-black paint job.

The twenty-six MH-47E models, introduced in 1991, incorporated all the features of the MH-47D but added terrain-following radar, improved avionics, Lycoming T55-L714 engines, an external rescue hoist, and, most noticeably, enlarged fuel tanks, which doubled the integral fuel capacity.

The latest model of special-operations Chinook is the MH-47G, which combines the new CH-47F airframe with the attributes of the MH-47E, including enlarged fuel tanks. Additionally, the MH-47G includes the special-operations Common Avionics Architecture System (CAAS) avionics package, as well as multimode radar with terrain following / terrain avoidance and weather detection. The MH-47G is equipped for use with Fast Rope Insertion and Extraction (FRIES) and Special Patrol Insertion & Extraction System (SPIES). Armament of the MH-47G is formidable, with two M134 miniguns as well as two M240D machine guns.

The MH-47 series was designed for use in special-forces operations, featuring a long refueling probe for in-flight fuel replenishment, a fast-rope rappeling system, and further improvements. Of the twelve MH-47Ds delivered starting in 1983, half were converted from CH-47As and the remainder from CH-47Cs. Also delivered starting in 1991 were the MH-47Es, a conversion from CH-47Cs, which had provisions for more fuel as well as terrain-following/avoidance radar. More recently, deliveries of the MH-47G began in 2004. The MH-47s were assigned to the 160th Special Operations Aviation Regiment (Airborne) "Nightstalkers," based at Fort Campbell, Kentucky. Here, an MH-47 hovers while special-forces troops leap off the ramp and into the water.

A US Army MH-47 Chinook, assigned to the 160th Special Operations Aviation Regiment, departs from the flight deck aboard the amphibious assault ship USS *Wasp* (LHD-1) during the ship's deck-landing qualification. The MH-47 Special Operations Aircraft is a long-distance, heavy-lift helicopter, which is equipped with aerial-refueling capability, a fast-rope rappeling system, and other upgrades of operations-specific equipment.

An MH-47 Chinook of the160th Special Operations Aviation Regiment (Airborne) lifts off from the flight deck of USS *Wasp* during the ship's deck-landing qualification on August 5, 2005. Markings were conspicuously absent from these special-ops helicopters.

During a training exercise off South Korea, an MH-47 from the 160th Special Operations Aviation Regiment (Airborne) is taking on fuel from a MC-130P Combat Shadow in March 2009. At the time, the 160th SOAR was deployed from Fort Lewis, Washington.

During an infiltration training exercise, members of the US Air Force's 23rd Special Tactics Squadron fitted out as frogmen jump off the lowered ramp of an MH-47 Chinook Helicopter at Wynnehaven Beach, Florida, on April 9, 2013.

An MH-47 from the 160th Special Operations Aviation Regiment (Airborne) hovers over water as crewmen toss a rope ladder off the ramp, to recover special-forces operators during an infiltration/exfiltration training mission during Foal Eagle 2009 in Korea.

| SPECIFICATIONS | | | | | | | | |
|---|---|---|---|---|---|---|---|---|
| | **CH-47A** | **CH-47B** | **CH-47C** | **CH-47D** | **CH-47F** | **MH-47D** | **MH-47E** | **MH-47G** |
| **DIMENSIONS** feet-inches | | | | | | | | |
| Length, rotors operating | 98' 1.3" | 98' 11" | 98' 11" | 98' 11" | 98' 11" | 98' 11" | 98' 11" | 98' 11" |
| Length, fuselage | 50' 9" | 50' 9" | 50' 9" | 50' 9" | 50' 9" | 52' 1" | 52' 1" | 52' 1" |
| Width over fuel tanks | 12' 5" | 12' 5" | 12' 5" | 12' 5" | 12' 5" | 12' 5" | 15' 8" | 15' 8" |
| Height (top of aft rotor head) | 18' 6" | 18' 6" | 18' 6" | 18' 6" | 18' 6" | 18' 6" | 18' 6" | 18' 6" |
| Rotor diameter | 59' 1.25" | 60' 0" | 60' 0" | 60' 0" | 60' 0" | 60' 0" | 60' 0" | 60' 0" |
| Wheelbase | 22' 10" | 22' 10" | 22' 10" | 22' 10" | 22' 10" | 22' 10" | 25' 10" | 25' 10" |
| Cabin length | 30' 6" | 30' 6" | 30' 6" | 30' 6" | 30' 6" | 30' 6" | 30' 6" | 30' 6" |
| Cabin width | 7' 6" | 7' 6" | 7' 6" | 7' 6" | 7' 6" | 7' 6" | 7' 6" | 7' 6" |
| Cabin height | 6' 6" | 6' 6" | 6' 6" | 6' 6" | 6' 6″ | 6' 6" | 6' 6" | 6' 6" |
| **FUEL** gals. | | | | | | | | |
| Integral | 621 | 621* | 1,100** | 1,034 | 1,034 | 1,034 | 2,068 | 2,068 |
| Auxiliary (max.) | none | none | none | 2,400 | 2,400 | 2,400 | 2,400 | 2,400 |
| In-flight refueling | no | no | no | no | no | yes | yes | yes |
| **WEIGHTS** lbs. | | | | | | | | |
| Empty weight | 18,288 | 19,676 | 21,586 | 23,729 | 24,000 | 23,729 | 26,918 | 26,918 |
| Maximum gross weight | 33,000 | 40,000 | 46,000 | 50,000 | 50,000 | 50,000 | 54,000 | 54,000 |
| **PERFORMANCE** | | | | | | | | |
| Max. cruise speed | 110 knots | 155 knots | 161 knots | 158 knots | 158 knots | 158 knots | 140 knots | 160 knots |
| Maximum speed | 130 knots | 165 knots | | 163 knots | 170 knots | 170 knots | 154 knots | 170 knots |
| Cruise speed (SL) | 110 knots | 140 knots | 150 knots | 130 knots | 130 knots | 130 knots | 140 knots | 130 knots |
| Service ceiling | 11,900 ft. | 16,300 ft. | 15,000 ft. | 20,000 ft. | 20,000 ft. | 20,000 ft. | 20,000 ft. | 20,000 ft. |
| Single hook capacity | 16,000 lbs. | 20,000 lbs. | 20,000 lbs. | 26,000 lbs. | 26,000 lbs. | 26,000 lbs. | 26,000 lbs. | 26,000 lbs. |
| Forward or aft hook | not applicable | not applicable | not applicable | 17,000 lbs. | 17,000 lbs. | 17,000 lbs. | 17,000 lbs. | 17,000 lbs. |
| **ENGINES** Shaft horsepower | | | | | | | | |
| Type | T55-L- 7C | T55-L- 7C | T55-L-11xcv | T55-L- 712A | T55-L- 714A | T55-L- 712A | T55-L- 714A | T55-L- 714A |
| Maximum power | 2,850 | 2,850 | 3,750 | 3,750 | 4,867 | 3,750 | 4,867 | 4,867 |
| Normal | 2,400 | 2,400 | 3,300 | 3,000 | 4,168 | 3,000 | 4,168 | 4,168 |
| Military power (30 min.) | 2,650 | 2,650 | 3,750 | 3,400 | 4,527 | 3,400 | 4,527 | 4,527 |
| Emergency | – | – | – | 4,500 | 5,069 | 4,500 | 5,069 | 5,069 |
| Rotor rpm | 230 | 225/230 | 235/245 | 225 | 225 | 225 | 225 | 225 |

* CH-47B aircraft with crash-resistant fuel tanks had a 566 gal. / 2,143-liter total capacity.
** CH-47C aircraft with crash-resistant fuel tanks had a 1,036 gal. / 3,922-liter total capacity.

CHAPTER 5

# The Chinook in Service

Before making their name in the Vietnam War, Chinook helicopters operated stateside in the early 1960s. This CH-47A, serial number 64-13122, making a flight along Manhattan Island, was delivered to the US Army on March 10, 1965.

Two US Army CH-47A Chinook medium helicopters are flying in formation during a training exercise at Fort Rucker on February 4, 1963. The closer Chinook was serial number 60-3450, the third production CH-47, which was delivered on June 29, 1962. *National Archives*

This rear view of the fourth production CH-47A Chinook, serial number 60-3450, illustrates a key identifying feature of the A model: the sharp rear vertical edge of the aft rotor pylon. Near the base of the pylon is the exhaust for the auxiliary power unit.

In 1963, CH-47A 61-2425 is airlifting a 2½-ton 6 × 6 cargo truck at McCoy Air Force Base, Florida, during an evaluation of the Chinook's ability to rapidly move missile batteries: "shoot-and-scoot," to establish a new emplacement before the enemy can hit back. *Army Aviation Museum*

Using the high-capacity hook on the belly, CH-47A, serial number 62-2119, is transporting a slung M56 Scorpion 90 mm self-propelled gun into a simulated combat area during training maneuvers at Fort Benning, Georgia, on July 10, 1964. *National Archives*

The US Army shipped CH-47As to the Republic of Vietnam in large numbers beginning with the shipment of 1st Cavalry Division (Air Mobile) Chinooks seen here, arriving aboard the carrier USS *Boxer* at Qui Nhon, Republic of Vietnam, on September 13, 1965. *National Archives*

Boeing Vertol CH-47As interspersed with Bell UH-1 helicopters are lined up on the flight deck of USS *Boxer* upon arrival at Qui Nhon, September 13, 1965. For the voyage, sealants and protective covers had been applied to the helicopters and the rotors had been removed. *National Archives*

CH-47A 64-13127 of 1st Cavalry Division (Air Mobile) is being spotted on the flight deck of USS *Boxer*. The helicopters were stripped of protective materials, the rotors were installed, systems were checked, and the Chinooks flew off from the deck for land. *National Archives*

A CH-47A is airlifting members of Company C, 2nd Battalion, 18th Infantry, to a site near Xa Cam My, Republic of Vietnam, on April 2, 1966, for Operation Abilene, a search-and-destroy mission. Chinooks in Vietnam were painted matte Olive Drab. *National Archives*

Chinooks quickly proved their worth as troop and cargo transporters in Vietnam. Here, a CH-47A is bringing supplies to Battery C, 2nd Battalion, 7th Artillery, during Operation Crazy Horse, a search-and-destroy mission in the Vinh Thanh Valley on May 25, 1966. *National Archives*

A CH-47A helicopter is carrying artillery ammunition in slings in order to resupply Battery C, 2nd Battalion, 19th Artillery, in the Vinh Thanh Valley on May 25, 1966. CH-47As soon proved to be underpowered for operations in the extreme heat of Vietnam. *National Archives*

Occasionally, a Chinook was the subject of an airlift instead of the instigator, as in this case of a Sikorsky CH-54 Tarhe helicopter transporting a CH-47A that had crashed to An Khe. The fuselage of the Chinook seems mostly intact, but both rotor pylons are missing. *National Archives*

On August 26, 1966, a CH-47A is about to take on a sling load of 105 mm howitzer ammunition at Ammunition Supply Point (ASP) Oasis for transport to an artillery unit in the field. A soldier on the ground is holding a sling, ready to attach it to the cargo hook. *National Archives*

In May 1966, three of the four ACH-47 gunships arrived in Vietnam with the 53rd Aviation Detachment, for evaluation in combat. Here, a trooper is loading ammunition for the 40 mm grenade launcher. The insignia of the 53rd Aviation Detachment (AD) is on the front rotor pylon. *Army Aviation Museum*

A member of the 53rd AD is checking the armor plates attached to the forward part of the fuselage of an ACH-47, to provide protection to the flight crew from small-arms fire. To the left is the 40 mm flex feed chute with its cover removed. *Army Aviation Museum*

The right-hand installation of an XM159 nineteen-round, 2.75-inch rocket-launcher pod and an M24A1 20 mm cannon on a Boeing Vertol ACH-47A in Vietnam is depicted. The pod is one round short of a full complement of nineteen of the 2.75-inch rockets loaded into the launcher pod. *Army Aviation Museum*

A member of the 53rd AD is making adjustments to the feed mechanism of an M24A1 20 mm cannon mounted on the right stub wing of an ACH-47A. These gunships were nicknamed "Guns A-Go-Go" and "Go-Go Birds." *Army Aviation Museum*

Two soldiers are loading 2.75-inch rockets into the right launcher pod of an ACH-47A, while two others look into a hatch on the right fuselage sponson, inside which is the transformer/rectifier cooling fan. To the right is a window-mounted .50-caliber machine gun. *National Archives*

Specialist 4th Class John Gunther, a .50-caliber gunner, loads a machine gun in the left side of an ACH-47A on September 21, 1966. Chromate green primer is on the upper part of the cargo compartment, while a gray paint is on the lower half. *National Archives*

A member of the 53rd Aviation Detachment (Field Evaluation) (Provisional) lugs an XM159 nineteen-round, 2.75-inch rocket-launcher pod on his shoulder while walking by an ACH-47A gunship that has a fully loaded nineteen-round rocket pod on its left stub wing. *National Archives*

"Easy Money" is the nickname painted in white on the fuselage aft of the cockpit of this ACH-47A being readied for a combat mission on September 21, 1966. The three ACH-47s were supporting the 1st Cavalry Division, lending fire support for ground troops. *National Archives*

An ACH-47A from the 53rd Aviation Detachment (Field Evaluation) (Provisional) is visible through the open window of another ACH-47A of the same unit during a combat mission on September 21, 1966. This unit evaluated ACH-47s from June to October 1966. *National Archives*

A .50-caliber machine gunner in an ACH-47A observes the ground below for enemy targets. Below the machine gun is a metal bin for channeling spent casings to the collection bag below it. To the right of the gun is its feed chute and ammunition box. *Army Aviation Museum*

These CH-47As of the 228th Aviation Battalion (Assault Support Helicopter), 1st Cavalry Division (Airmobile), are engaged in a resupply mission in support of Operation Thayer on September 28, 1966. On the ground are 500-gallon portable fuel tanks. *National Archives*

On September 28, 1966, the CH-47A helicopter pad at An Khe, Republic of Vietnam, is viewed facing to the south. These Chinooks of 228th Aviation Battalion (Assault Support Helicopter) were being prepared to resupply ground troops in Operation Thayer. *National Archives*

This CH-47, serial number 61-3144, from Company B, 228th Aviation Battalion, is framed in the round window of another Chinook on September 28, 1966. Both helicopters were standing by prior to commencing a resupply mission for troops in Operation Thayer. *National Archives*

A ¼-ton truck is disembarking from CH-47A, serial number 66-0069, from the 228th Aviation Battalion in support of Operation Thayer, a 1st Cavalry Division (Airmobile) search-and-destroy mission conducted 45 kilometers northeast of An Khe, on September 28, 1966. *National Archives*

During Operation Irving, a 1st Cavalry Division search-and-destroy operation against the Viet Cong in Phu My Province on October 10 and 11, 1966, this CH-47A, serial number 64-13124, is picking up members of the 8th Cavalry Regiment for airlift into combat. *National Archives*

Troops of the 1st Engineer Battalion, 1st Cavalry Division, rappel from a CH-47A during Operation Cedar Falls, a massive search-and-destroy mission in the Iron Triangle in January 1967. They would use chain saws and explosives to clear a landing zone. *National Archives*

CH-47As, with their capacity to carry many stretcher or ambulatory patients, often served as medevac helicopters. This Chinook has just brought a wounded soldier to a base, where the awaiting ambulance will take him to a field hospital, on June 6, 1967. *National Archives*

Chinooks in Vietnam assisted artillery units to move their pieces into firing positions and then quickly move them to new positions. Here, a Chinook of the 213th Aviation Company is airlifting a 105 mm howitzer during Operation Billings on June 10, 1967. *National Archives*

On July 6, 1967, a CH-47 is preparing to airlift supplies back to the base at Cu Chi during Operation Kole Kole, a 25th Infantry Division search-and-destroy mission. *To the left*, a soldier is standing on a pack of supplies, ready to attach the sling to the cargo hook. *National Archives*

A CH-47A, serial number 65-8023, is airlifting a 105 mm howitzer to a base camp at Tan Uyen, near Long Binh, in mid-August 1967. On the aft rotor pylon is a white, red, and white flash. The upper part of the ramp is retracted into the lower half of the ramp. *National Archives*

A CH-47 Chinook is lifting supplies for the construction of a forward base camp at the intersections of two canals during Operation Shelby on August 21 or 22, 1967. On the aft rotor pylon is a white, pentagonal insignia with a diagonal red stripe across it. *National Archives*

In a companion view to the preceding photo, taken on September 21 or 22, 1967, during Operation Shelby, a CH-47 is bringing in a sling load of sandbags for the construction of defenses at a forward base. A white "X" is on the aft rotor pylon. *National Archives*

A CH-47A from the "Long Horns," B Company, 228th Assault Support Helicopter Battalion (ASHB), 1st Cavalry Division, unloads troops from C Company, 1st Battalion, 50th Mech, at Landing Zone (LZ) Quick. The troops are beginning a search-and-destroy mission in the Cay Giep Mountains, Vietnam, in October 1967. *National Archives*

Members of an ARVN unit are preparing to fasten a slung 155 mm howitzer to a hovering CH-47 in January 1969. The presence of a strake on the fuselage sponson identifies this Chinook as a CH-47B or CH-47C. A gunner next to an M60 machine gun looks out the door. *National Archives*

A soldier is securing the "doughnut ring" of a sling to the cargo hook of a Chinook medium helicopter hovering just feet off the ground. The sling contains packing tubes for heavy artillery ammunition; unpacked projectiles are on the ground to the left. *National Archives*

This CH-47A, serial number 65-7990, is being prepared for transporting supplies from the helipad of Company C, 3rd Signal Battalion, 45 miles out of Saigon, to troops atop Hill 837, Nui Chua Chan. Chinooks were able to resupply the most-isolated outposts. *National Archives*

The Chinook helicopter to the right is being refueled at the base of the 228th Supply and Service Company, 277th Supply and Service Battalion, Tay Ninh, Republic of Vietnam, while another Chinook is preparing to land, on April 19, 1970. *National Archives*

A CH-47 Chinook is stirring up considerable dust as it is about to touch down at LZ Bronco during the incursion into Cambodia in late June 1970. The helicopter was on a medevac mission to extract wounded troops for treatment at a rear-area hospital. *National Archives*

Soldiers are securing a sling full of materiel to the cargo hook of a CH-47A at LZ Bronco in Cambodia, for return to Vietnam on June 23 or 24, 1970. Cargo handlers found that the area directly under the low-hovering Chinook was surprisingly calm. *National Archives*

The 1st Cavalry Division (Airmobile) crest is on the aft rotor pylon of this CH-47A from which troops are disembarking at LZ Ramada in Cambodia on June 23 or 24, 1970. They are pushing what appears to be a mechanical mule down the ramp. *National Archives*

Troopers from the 8th Cavalry Regiment, 1st Cavalry Division, are boarding a CH-47A, serial number 66-0074, at Fire Support Base Condor for transport back to Vietnam during the Cambodian Incursion, on June 27, 1970. A white-blue-white flash is on the aft pylon. *National Archives*

A Chinook is about to lift a sling load of crates and cargo at Fire Base David, operated by the 1st Brigade, 1st Cavalry Division (Airmobile), in Cambodia in mid-July 1970. The absence of strakes on the rears of the sponsons marks this as a CH-47A. *National Archives*

Two slings full of cargo are fastened to the cargo hook of a CH-47A Chinook lifting off from Fire Base David in Cambodia in mid-July 1970. A major portion, if not the majority, of the cargo the Chinooks airlifted in the Vietnam War was slung loads. *National Archives*

Chinooks were called on to recover and transport downed US aircraft back to air bases, for repair or salvaging. Here, a CH-47 is airlifting a Bell UH-1 helicopter from the 25th Infantry Division that was downed north of Nui Ba Den in the first half of August 1970. *National Archives*

Fitted with ski landing gear, a CH-47 Chinook helicopter is about to land on Trident Glacier, south of Fort Greely, Alaska, during a training exercise for operating on glaciers conducted by the Northern Warfare Training Center, Fort Greely, in September 1970. *National Archives*

Sometimes the Chinook was put to use transporting nonmilitary cargo, such as this CH-47, which has just brought Bob Hope's Golddiggers song-and-dance troupe to 2nd Infantry Division Recreation Center No. 1 in Korea in December 1970. *National Archives*

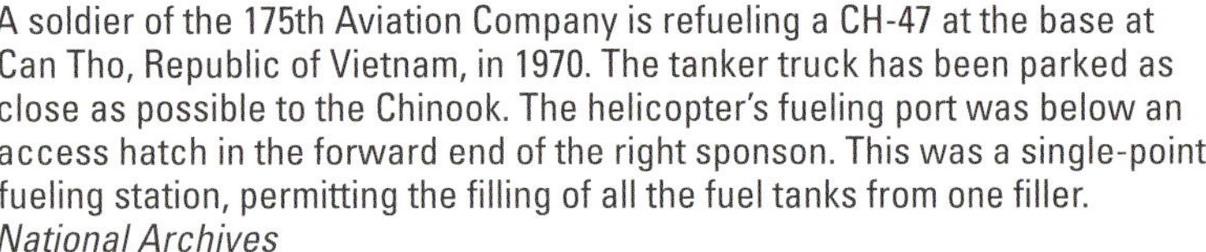

A soldier of the 175th Aviation Company is refueling a CH-47 at the base at Can Tho, Republic of Vietnam, in 1970. The tanker truck has been parked as close as possible to the Chinook. The helicopter's fueling port was below an access hatch in the forward end of the right sponson. This was a single-point fueling station, permitting the filling of all the fuel tanks from one filler. *National Archives*

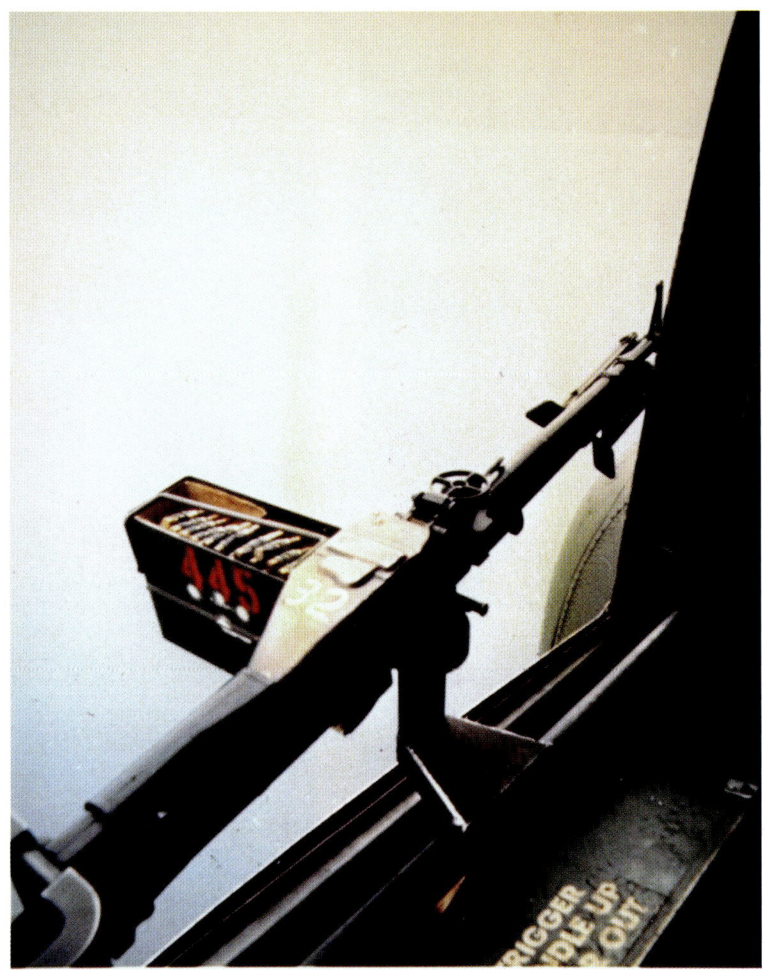


Window-mounted M60D 7.62 mm machine guns in CH-47 helicopters gave the aircrews the means of laying down suppressive fire when approaching or departing from contested landing zones. The M60D was designed for flexible mounts in vehicles and aircraft and was equipped with two spade grips (*bottom left*) rather than the M60's pistol grip. A fold-down ring sight was installed on the receiver. *National Archives*

A crew chief from the 147th Aviation Company stands by, ready to guide a CH-47 Chinook helicopter out of a revetment in preparation for a mission at Can Tho, Republic of Vietnam, during 1970. Can Tho was a major airbase in the Mekong delta. *National Archives*

A member of Battery B, 3rd Battalion, 82nd Artillery Regiment, looks skyward as a CH-47A Chinook descends for a landing at Fire Base Center, Republic of Vietnam, in 1970. Goggles, as worn by the artilleryman, were desirable safety equipment when working around a helicopter landing zone. The dark spot on the belly of the Chinook marks the location of the cargo hook. *National Archives*

In Vietnam, the Chinook helicopter seemingly had a thousand uses. Here, a CH-47 from the 213th Assault Helicopter Company, 145th Aviation Battalion, is hovering over a pond, collecting large buckets of water to dump on a grass fire, on July 5, 1971. *National Archives*

A helicopter from the 213th Assault Helicopter Company, 145th Aviation Battalion, releases water from two buckets onto a grass fire in the Republic of Vietnam on July 5, 1971. A red-and-white roundel, possibly with another outer ring, is on the aft pylon. *National Archives*

Troops are loading their baggage in a Chinook during an evacuation of civilians and nonessential US military personnel at Kontum, Republic of Vietnam, on May 3, 1972. The tail number, 8541, likely indicates that this was CH-47C serial number 67-18541. *National Archives*

Troops are unloading supplies from a CH-47 at a base camp during training maneuvers on the Eklatuna ice field, Fort Richardson, Alaska, in January 1973. High-visibility orange paint is on the front and the rear of the Chinook as an aid to potential rescuers. *National Archives*

A CH-47B or C from the 213th Aviation Company (Assault Support Helicopter), based at Camp Humphreys, Republic of Korea, is being positioned to lift a TRAC 120 communications van from the Highpoint Signal Site, near Puonteak, on June 7, 1973. *National Archives*

An emergency repair shelter covers the aft part of a CH-47 at Fort Wainwright, Alaska, on April 24, 1974. The US Army Arctic Test Center was conducting evaluations on this new shelter. An external heater unit is pumping warm air into the shelter. *National Archives*

Army paratroopers in winter camouflage parkas prepare for a static-line jump from a CH-47 Chinook during Exercise Jack Frost '75 out of Eielson Air Force Base, Alaska, in January 1975. The quilted soundproofing insulation in the compartment is noticeable. *National Archives*

During an annual service practice at an Eighth Army range near Daechon Beach, Republic of Korea, in the spring of 1976, a CH-47 Chinook is airlifting by sling a Ryan Firebee target drone back to its helipad. The Firebee weighed about 1,500 pounds empty. *National Archives*

A CH-47C is landing a Chaparral antiaircraft missile launcher during a field exercise in the Kaiserlautern Area, West Germany, around October 1976. This was the first time the launchers had been airlifted to a launch site under operational conditions. *National Archives*

In the distance, low over the Cowhouse River, a CH-47 Chinook from the 6th Cavalry is approaching a pontoon bridge under construction. This was during Operation Gallant Crew '77, a joint-services exercise at Fort Hood, Texas, in March 1977.

A CH-47 Chinook helicopter serving with the 6th Cavalry lowers a section of a pontoon bridge into the Cowhouse River during the joint-services Operation Gallant Crew '77. Using a medium-lift helicopter in this manner made for relatively quick bridge building.

On July 17, 1978, a CH-47 is lifting a stripped 6 × 6 truck as part of a test of the effect of the slung load on an AN/ASN-128 Lightweight Doppler Navigation System installed in the Chinook. This helicopter also was equipped with a prototype multiple-hook system. *National Archives*

Chinooks amassed an impressive record of recovering downed aircraft in Vietnam and after the war, stateside and around the world. Here, a CH-47B or C is airlifting a UH-1 medevac helicopter that had crashed during a rescue mission in the Colorado Rockies on August 15, 1978. The number 505 is painted in white on the flattened trailing edge of the aft rotor pylon of the Chinook. The UH-1's rotors are secured with cords to keep them from whipping around. *National Archives*

Army mechanics are servicing the engine and rotor of a CH-47. The engine access panels are hinged forward. Above the engine, a stressed-metal access hatch serves as a work platform for the kneeling mechanic. Access doors on the front of the pylon are open.

A mechanic is making adjustments to the left engine's quick-disconnect shelf: a fitting attached to the bottom of the engine that contains quick-release couplings for engine wiring, fuel, and hydraulic components, enabling rapid change-outs of the engine.

During Exercise Sentry Castle '81 at Fort Drum, New York, in July 1981, an Army CH-47A, as indicated by the lack of strakes and the sharp leading edge of the aft pylon, is in a hover as an Aggressor Forces M48A5 main battle tank advances through a field.

A CH-47C Chinook helicopter (note the pitot tube on the nose), numbered 526 on the forward rotor pylon, has landed with supplies at the base encampment area of the Korean Tactical Range in February 1982. A black-cat insignia is on the aft rotor pylon.

The same CH-47C seen in the preceding photo is in a low-level hover during a resupply mission to the base encampment area of the Korean Tactical Range in February 1982. This Chinook had several tan-colored skin panels in addition to the overall Olive Drab.

A US Army M151 MUTT with a trailer hitched to it is backing off the ramp of an Army Reserve CH-47A Chinook, serial number 65-8017, at Landing Zone Iron during Gallant Eagle '82, a desert-warfare training exercise at Fort Irwin, California, in April 1982.

Three CH-47 Chinook helicopters are flying in formation over an airbase during Exercise Ocean Venture '82, a joint air, sea, and ground readiness exercise in the Caribbean in April and May 1982. Flare dispensers are visible, jutting from the rears of the fuselages.

A CH-47C Chinook helicopter descends for a landing at Giessen Army Air Field, West Germany, during Exercise Reforger '81 in October 1981. A white number 677 is visible on the round window in the fuselage above the forward landing gear.

Members of Battery A, 2nd Battalion, 31st Field Artillery, hook a sling from an M198 155 mm howitzer to cargo hooks on a CH-47B or C during Exercise Eagle Strike III at Fort Campbell, Kentucky, in December 1982. The M198 howitzer weighs 15,772 pounds.

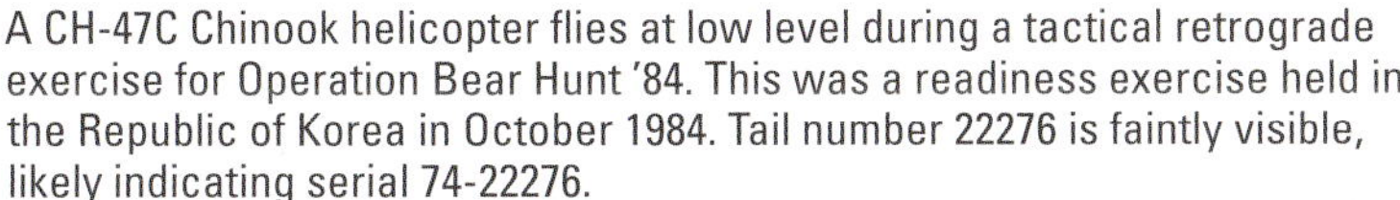

A CH-47C Chinook helicopter flies at low level during a tactical retrograde exercise for Operation Bear Hunt '84. This was a readiness exercise held in the Republic of Korea in October 1984. Tail number 22276 is faintly visible, likely indicating serial 74-22276.

Members of a mortar team from the 1st Battalion, 21st Infantry, 25th Infantry Division, prepare to board a CH-47 Chinook helicopter for a practice air assault during the joint South Korean / US training exercise Team Spirit '84 in March 1984.

A CH-47C is about to lift an M102 105 mm howitzer off the ground during the joint US/Honduran field-training Exercise Ahuas Tara II (Big Pine) in May 1984. Near the top of the aft rotor pylon is a blue silhouette of a porpoise, with "FLIPPER" written above it.

This photograph of a CH-47C Chinook was taken at Sainte-Mère-Église on or around June 6, 1984, while it was participating in a ceremony commemorating the fortieth anniversary of D-day, the Allied invasion of Europe. Red crew seats are visible through the windows.

NASA, in cooperation with the US Army, operated a CH-47B in a program of tests of improved flight-control systems at Ames Research Center during 1985. The tail number 737 was applied to this helicopter, and it was painted overall in white, with dark-blue trim. *NASA*

A view of a mechanic working on the forward rotor system provides an excellent view of the access doors of the pylon, which doubled as work platforms. The transmission mount and control mechanisms within the pylon were coated with zinc chromate primer.

Men of the 320th General Support Aviation Company perform maintenance on a CH-47 during disaster relief in Colombia after the eruption of a volcano. Two of the men are standing on a built-in work platform. The hinged spine containing the driveshaft is open.

A US Army CH-47D Chinook takes off from the helipad of the battleship USS *Iowa* (BB-61) in January 1987, while doing duty transporting personnel and supplies while the ship is visiting Puerto Cortés, Honduras, for a civic-action program.

Three CH-47 Chinook helicopters are engaged in airlifting artillery pieces in support of air-assault units during a joint US Air Force and US Army air-drop/air-assault exercise at the Darlington County Airport, South Carolina, in October 1987.

The same three CH-47 Chinook helicopters shown in the preceding photo are seen from a different angle during an airlift of artillery pieces at the Darlington County Airport. Chinooks were instrumental in giving artillery batteries the ability to "shoot and scoot."

A CH-47 Chinook helicopter is descending for a landing onto a temporary helipad at the 129th Evacuation Hospital field station during the mass-casualty phase of the joint US / South Korean Exercise Team Spirit '87 at Osan, Republic of Korea, during 1987.

Medics from the 129th Evacuation Hospital carry wounded soldiers on a stretcher from the rear of a CH-47 during the mass-casualty phase of Team Spirit '87. Twenty-four stretcher patients could be carried in the CH-47, in three tiers per side, four stretchers high per tier.

Members of the 129th Evacuation Hospital prepare to remove simulated stretcher patients from a CH-47 during Team Spirit '87. The outboard sides of the stretcher rails were supported by rigid brackets, while the inboard sides were held by straps and clamps.

A CH-47D Chinook helicopter takes off from a clearing at Palmerola Air Base, Honduras, during the joint Honduran/US Exercise Cabanas '88. The silhouettes of the three cargo hooks on the belly, a characteristic of the CH-47Ds, are visible.

As part of a foreign-assistance road construction project by members of the West Virginia Army National Guard deployed to the Puenta Grande area in Honduras in March 1983, a CH-47D Chinook helicopter has two lift cables rigged to a section of concrete culvert. Next, the Chinook will serve as a flying crane, airlifting the culvert section to the point where it is needed.

A CH-47D, recognizable by the large opening in the front of the aft pylon, is airlifting by slings four potable-water bladders to the field during Operation Golden Pheasant in Honduras in March 1988. The bladders are marked "DRINKING WATER ONLY."

A ground crewman is hauling a fuel hose up to a CH-47 Chinook in preparation for refueling the helicopter at Bradshaw Air Field, Pohakuloa Training Area, Hawaii, during the 21st Infantry Division's annual field exercises in 1988.

A CH-47C Chinook helicopter equipped with skis on the landing gear is engaged in airlifting 105 mm howitzers of Battery A, 4th Battalion, 11th Field Artillery, to Drop Zone Husky during combined Army–Air Force live fire exercises Calfex IV at the Yukon Command Training Site, Eielson Air Force Base, Alaska, in September 1988.

In a companion photo to the preceding one, a CH-47 is lowering a 105 mm howitzer assigned to Battery A, 4th Battalion, 11th Field Artillery, onto Drop Zone Husky during Calfex IV, combined Army–Air Force live-fire Exercises at the Yukon Command Training Site, Eielson Air Force Base, Alaska. Skis are mounted on the landing gear for possible operations on snow.

In the foreground, a member of a ground-support crew, wearing an orange-and-yellow high-visibility vest and a Kevlar helmet, is signaling to the pilot of a CH-47 Chinook who is approaching to attempt to retrieve the container in the background. This operation transpired during Exercise Team Spirit '89 in the Republic of Korea.

In a continuation of the operation depicted in the preceding view, the member of the ground support crew has arms stretched out to signal the pilot of a CH-47 Chinook helicopter while he maneuvers close to the ground, to enable the two handlers under the helicopter to secure a container to the copter's cargo hook.

Two US Army CH-47 Chinook helicopters, including in the foreground a CH-47D with the number 57 in a window, are lifting slung M102 105 mm light towed howitzers during the joint-service exercise Ocean Venture '90 in Puerto Rico in January 1990.

Members of 1st Battalion, 325th Airborne Infantry Regiment, are securing by slings an M102 105 mm towed howitzer and an M998 HMMWV to a CH-47D after a firing demonstration for Saudi Arabian national guardsmen during Operation Desert Shield.

In a photo probably taken minutes after the preceding view, a CH-47D is airlifting an M998 HMMWV with an M102 105 mm howitzer hitched to it. The vehicle and howitzer were from the 1st Battalion, 325th Airborne Infantry Regiment.

Through a haze of dust, US Army CH-47 Chinook helicopters are taking off from a site in Saudi Arabia on a mission during Operation Desert Shield—the buildup phase prior to the expulsion of Iraqi forces from Kuwait—from August 2, 1990, to January 16, 1991.

Two soldiers of the 82nd Airborne Division observe a Chinook preparing to touch down at a site in Saudi Arabia during Operation Desert Shield. This is a CH-47D, as indicated by the three cargo hooks and the opening in the front of the aft rotor pylon.

A line of CH-47 Chinooks (*left*) and UH-60 Blackhawk helicopters (*right*) assembled at Jacksonville, Florida, are clad in protective covers, except for the landing gear, in preparation for shipment to the Middle East in support of Operation Desert Shield in August 1990.

Kurdish refugees have a look at a US Army CH-47D that will transport them to a new refugee camp in northern Iraq in April 1991. Above the two pitot tubes on the nose are radar-warning antennas. Below the nose are retractable, aimable taxiing lights.

In May 1991, a gunner in a US Army CH-47 Chinook stands by next to a window-mounted .50-caliber machine gun during operations in support of Operation Provide Comfort, efforts to aid Kurdish refugees who fled the forces of Saddam Hussein in northern Iraq in the wake of Operation Desert Storm. He is leaning on the ammunition box for the gun, containing 100 rounds of linked .50-caliber ammo.

The same window gunner featured in the preceding photo is seen at another moment, manning a .50-caliber M2 machine gun. This mount is in the forward left window of the cargo compartment; to the far right, the passageway to the cockpit is visible.

Members of the 24th Forward Support Battalion, 24th Infantry Division (Mechanized), are securing a sling attached to an HMMWV to a CH-47 Chinook during sling-load training at the Remagen Drop Zone, Fort Stewart, Georgia, in January 1996.

Soldiers from A Company, 4th Battalion 87th Infantry, 25th Infantry Division, are boarding a CH-47 on March 3, 1995, after conducting a company-size patrol of LeBorgne, Haiti, and vicinity in a peacekeeping operation, Uphold Democracy.

A ground crewman is signaling the pilot of a Royal Air Force Chinook helicopter about to depart from Aviano Air Base, Italy, during Operation Joint Endeavor, the code name for the one-year mandate beginning on December 20, 1995, for the NATO-led Implementation Force (IFOR), a multinational peacekeeping force, to operate in Bosnia and Herzegovina. The RAF's blue-and-red roundel is above the first and second round windows of the cargo compartment.

A US Army CH-47 Chinook is lifting an M119 105 mm howitzer for transport from Camp Lejeune to Camp McKall, North Carolina, for the final phase of Combined Joint Task Force Exercise '96 (CJTFEX 96), a training exercise in April and May 1996.

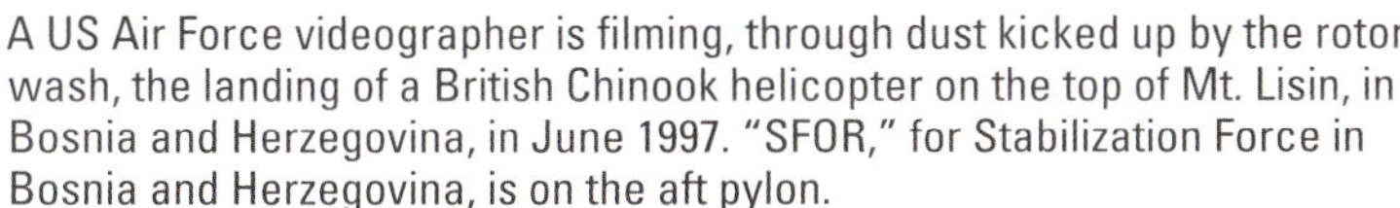

A US Air Force videographer is filming, through dust kicked up by the rotor wash, the landing of a British Chinook helicopter on the top of Mt. Lisin, in Bosnia and Herzegovina, in June 1997. "SFOR," for Stabilization Force in Bosnia and Herzegovina, is on the aft pylon.

Army and Air Force personnel are maneuvering a pylon and rotor assembly from a Army National Guard CH-47D Chinook down the ramp of a C-5B Galaxy at the airport at Timehri, Guyana, during New Horizon '97, a joint US-Guyana humanitarian exercise.

A soldier kneels in the foreground while two structural engineers from the 820th Red Horse Squadron, Nellis Air Force Base, Nevada, prepare to attach two sling rings onto a CH-47D Chinook in order to airlift a tractor secured to a flatbed trailer. The scene was at Kumaka, Guyana, in July 1997, and the destination of the Chinook and its load was Camp Stephenson, Timerhi, Guyana. This event was during a combined humanitarian and civic-assistance exercise of US and Guyanese forces.

During the joint US-Guyanese exercise depicted in the preceding photo, two soldiers attach two sling harnesses of supplies to an Iowa Army National Guard CH-47 Chinook helicopter. The supplies were to be airlifted to a remote site in Guyana.

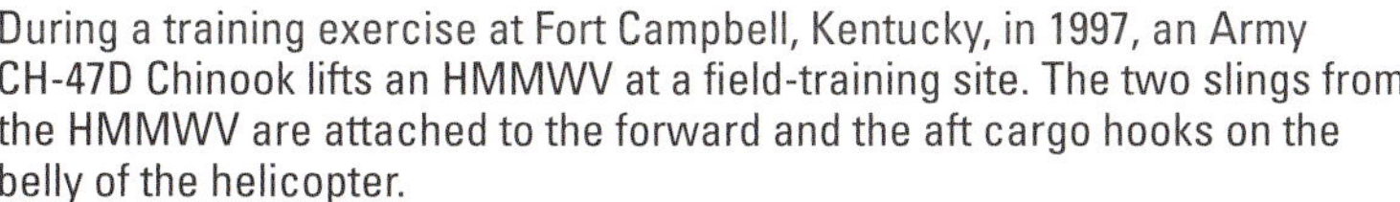

During a training exercise at Fort Campbell, Kentucky, in 1997, an Army CH-47D Chinook lifts an HMMWV at a field-training site. The two slings from the HMMWV are attached to the forward and the aft cargo hooks on the belly of the helicopter.

A view through the center cargo hatch in the belly of a CH-47 attached to the 49th Armored Division, Texas National Guard, shows, *in the foreground*, the radius bar from which the hook is suspended, below which is an HMMWV being transported by slings.

During a sling-load practice exercise at Fort Hood, Texas, in June 2000, soldiers from the 21st Combat Support Hospital, 1st Medical Brigade, are attaching a sling from a High-Mobility Multipurpose Wheeled Vehicle (HMMWV) to the center-bay hoist of a hovering CH-47D Chinook from the 49th Armored Division, Texas National Guard. The Chinook gave motorized troops the ability to extricate themselves and their vehicle from an area quickly, or to be airlifted over obstacles.

The two members of the 21st Combat Support Hospital seen in the preceding photo are jumping clear of the HMMWV now that they have completed the attachment of the sling to the CH-47D and the helicopter is about to ascend, at Fort Hood, Texas, in June 2006.

During a June 2000 field exercise at Fort Hood, Texas, featuring simulated wounded troops, medics from the 21st Combat Support Hospital await the signal to load their casualties into the CH-47D Chinook helicopter in the background.

A US Army MH-47 Chinook operated by Company B, 2nd Battalion, 160th Special Operations Aviation Regiment, based at Fort Campbell, Kentucky, is employing its winch to pull a downed aircrew member from the 128th Air Refueling Wing from Lake Michigan during part of Exercise Whitetail 2001, a water-rescue exercise conducted on Lake Michigan and in Wisconsin in August 2001.

Two US Army CH-47 Chinooks are parked on a hardstand at the Bird International Airport, Antigua, during the Tradewinds '02 Field Training Exercise on April 11, 2002. The numbers 69 (*foreground*) and 00 are marked on the trailing edges of the pylons.

This Chinook from Company G, 140th Aviation, Nevada Army National Guard, seen at Bird International Airport during Tradewinds '02, was CH-47D serial number 92-00287, which had been converted to a D model from CH-47A serial number 62-02131.

A row of US Army CH-47 Chinook helicopters are parked on a ramp at Bird International Airport in April 2002. On their sides, and particularly noticeable to the far right, are blister windows, for better visibility; these began to be installed on Chinooks by 1984.

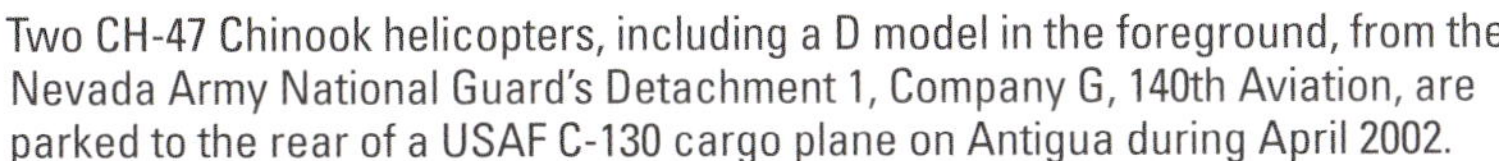
Two CH-47 Chinook helicopters, including a D model in the foreground, from the Nevada Army National Guard's Detachment 1, Company G, 140th Aviation, are parked to the rear of a USAF C-130 cargo plane on Antigua during April 2002.

Members of Bravo Company, 2nd Battalion, 20th Special Forces Group (Airborne), Maryland Army National Guard, load equipment onto a Chinook helicopter in preparation for returning home from Antigua at the conclusion of Tradewinds '02.

Crew members from Detachment 1, Company G, 140th Aviation, are performing routine maintenance on a CH-47D Chinook at Bird International Airport, Antigua, during Tradewinds '02 in April 2002. The number 69 is marked in white on the front of the forward rotor pylon. The fold-down access doors on the pylons serve as handy work platforms.

Soldiers of Bravo Company, 2nd Battalion, 20th Special Forces Group (Airborne), are beginning to disembark from a Chinook upon landing at the Robert Bradshaw International Airport, St. Kitts Island, during the Tradewinds '02 exercise in April 2002.

Regardless of location, maintenance of the helicopters is a priority. On Antigua during the Tradewinds '02 exercises on Antigua in April 2002, mechanics from Detachment 1, Company G, 140th Aviation, are performing maintenance on the aft drivetrain.

Two members of Detachment 1, Company G, 140th Aviation, are hooking a pair of M149 400-gallon "Water Buffalo" tank trailers to a hovering CH-47D Chinook at Bird International Airport during the Tradewinds '02 field training exercise on Antigua.

In a companion image to the preceding photo, a soldier is about to secure a sling clevis to the forward hook on the belly of a CH-47D during Tradewinds '02 on Antigua, April 2002. All three cargo hooks are in view, including the large center one in an open hatch.

In a continuation of the operation shown in the preceding photo, connections of the slings from the two M-149 Water Buffaloes to the cargo hooks on the CH-47D are complete, and the Chinook soon will be taking off, airlifting the two-trailer load to its destination.

During a May 3, 2003, training mission, troopers from Troop B, 9th Cavalry, 3rd Brigade Combat Team, 4th Infantry Division, are about to jump from the rear of a Chinook, tail number 0-24355, hovering over Townsend Reservoir at Fort Carson, Colorado.

In a continuation of the action depicted in the preceding photo, members of Troop B, 9th Cavalry, have jumped from the CH-47 helicopter into the undoubtedly chilly water of Townsend Reservoir. Water-insertion training was essential for light-cavalry units.

Civilians have been returned to their village, Deh Rawood, Afghanistan, by a US Army CH-47 Chinook after being treated for wounds suffered in an accidental bombing during Operation Enduring Freedom on August 2, 2002. A white number 326 is on a round window.

A US Army CH-47 is landing to refuel near the settlement of Khowst, Afghanistan, before transporting soldiers to Narizah, Afghanistan, to conduct a cordon search during Operation Mountain Sweep, a major US military offensive, on August 22, 2002.

Seeming conspicuous among the gray Navy aircraft, a US Army MH-47 Special Operations Force helicopter, deployed from Okinawa, is secured to the flight deck of USS *Kitty Hawk* (CV-63) as part of the aircrew's carrier qualifications, in November 2002.

An Army MH-47 hovers above Navy F/A-18 Hornets parked on the flight deck of USS *Kitty Hawk* as it prepares to land on the flight deck, as part of an approach-training and carrier-qualification program conducted in conjunction with the US Navy.

Soldiers assigned to Task Force 44 and the 924th Korean Medical Hospital are filing out from a CH-47D in the village of Aroki, Afghanistan, to conduct medical, dental, and veterinarian services for the locals during Operation Enduring Freedom in February 2003.

A US Army Chinook is approaching to evacuate a team of soldiers from the 3rd Battalion, 505th Infantry, from the village of Gangikhel, Afghanistan, after they completed missions to seek enemy forces' weapon caches during Operation Enduring Freedom.

US Army first lieutenant Aaron Van Zant, a Chinook helicopter pilot serving with the California Army National Guard, checks the right rear landing gear of his helicopter before the opening of the Western Air and Space Show at Vandenberg Air Force Base, California, on October 31, 2004. Some of the access panels on the sponson are open or removed.

In the aftermath of Hurricane Katrina, members of a FEMA (Federal Emergency Management Agency) search-and-rescue team, *right*, are preparing inflatable rafts prior to boarding a CH-47 Chinook assigned to Company B, 5th Battalion, 159th Aviation Regiment, Army National Guard, near Empire, Louisiana, on September 2, 2005. This regiment, based at Fort Eustis, Virginia, was the first Army Reserve unit mobilized for the recovery efforts. The Chinook is numbered "208" on the rear of the aft pylon.

Marines hook a sling load of food supplies to a US Army CH-47 during a relief operation in Pakistan on February 27, 2006. An Army aircrewman in the center cargo-hook hatch, commonly called the "hellhole," is assisting the Marines in the operation.

In a dramatic overhead view revealing rare details of the top of a CH-47D Chinook, the crew is preparing to unload cargo at a landing zone during a relief operation to assist victims of a severe earthquake in northern Pakistan, on October 12, 2005.

Specialist Matthew Patterson, a CH-47F crew chief from Company B, 4th Aviation Regiment, Combat Aviation Brigade (CAB), checks a gun mount at Camp Taji, Iraq, on July 8, 2008. The CAB was the first aviation brigade to field the CH-47F in Iraq. *DVIDS*

In a close-up of the left side of the forward part of a Chinook, Brig. Gen. Andrew W. O'Donnell Jr., commanding general of the 3rd Marine Aircraft Wing (Forward), is in the copilot's seat on June 8, 2010. In the window to the right is an M134 minigun mount. *DVIDS*

In Afghanistan on June 8, 2010, Sgt. Maj. Anthony Spadaro, 3rd Marine Aircraft Wing (Forward), is being briefed on operating a window-mounted M134 minigun in a CH-47 Chinook. This minigun had a rate of fire of 2,000 or 4,000 rounds per minute. *DVIDS*

A GI assigned to Company B, 2nd Battalion, 211th General Support Aviation Battalion, is standing by a machine gun mount on the cabin door of a Chinook at Camp Taji, Iraq, on February 13, 2011. The weapon is an M240D 7.62 mm machine gun on a door/window mount.

Members of the Logistical Support Team, 2nd Battalion, 1st Infantry Regiment, 2nd Stryker Brigade Combat Team, 2nd Infantry Division, are securing a disabled CH-47 helicopter, registration number 87-00111, on the semitrailer of a Stryker Recovery System at a site in Arghandab, Kandahar Province, Afghanistan, in August 2012. A mobile crane stands by to the right to assist in the lifting. The Chinook had crashed on its right side on August 12, when the flight crew lost visibility because of a dust cloud while attempting to land. No personnel perished in the crash.

Two CH-47F Chinooks from Company H, 1st Battalion, 214th Aviation Regiment, 12th Combat Aviation Brigade, take off to pick up air-assault troops during NATO Exercise Trident Juncture 2015, in Zaragoza, Spain, on November 3, 2015. *DVIDS*

A soldier from Bravo Company, 2-238 General Support Aviation Battalion, South Carolina Army National Guard, is refueling a CH-47 at McEntire Joint National Guard Base, South Carolina, during a statewide response to Hurricane Matthew in October 2016. *DVIDS*

A member of Company B, 3rd Battalion, 238th General Support Aviation Regiment, an Army Reserve unit based in Grand Ledge, Michigan, is pressure-washing CH-47F, serial number 11-08830, with a marking for the Ohio National Guard, in preparation for an inspection at Bagram Airfield, Afghanistan, on December 29, 2015. On the rear of the engine nacelle is an IRSS (Infrared Suppression System), for reducing the engine exhausts' contribution to the infrared signature of the aircraft. On the front of the nacelle is a foreign-object cone.

Two men from the 82nd Airborne Division Artillery strain to lift the sling rings to secure a M777A2 howitzer to a cargo hook on the belly of a hovering CH-47F Chinook assigned to 3rd General Support Aviation Battalion, during a field exercise at Fort Bragg, North Carolina, on July 19, 2016. The right pitot tube is the double-probe type that was a key exterior characteristic of the CH-47F. *DVIDS*

Troopers from 1st Cavalry Division's Resolute Support Sustainment Brigade hook up a shipping container to a CH-47 at Bagram Airfield, Afghanistan, in October 2016. It was crucial to ground the hooks before attaching the container, to prevent static-electrical shock. *DVIDS*

A soldier adjusts the aft rotor pylon of a CH-47F Chinook, serial number 13-08149, at Hunter Army Airfield, Fort Stewart, Georgia, prior to a sling-load mission on November 6, 2016. Stenciled in yellow on the rotor blade is its serial number. *DVIDS*

In the Gulf of Aden in November 2016, a sailor secures with chocks and chains a US Army CH-57F Chinook on the flight deck of the amphibious dock landing ship USS *Whidbey Island* (LSD-41), supporting Fifth Fleet maritime and theater security operations. *DVIDS*

Soldiers from Task Force Flying Dragons, 16th Combat Aviation Brigade, 7th Infantry Division, are performing maintenance on a CH-47F Chinook, serial number 07-08744, at Bagram Airfield, Afghanistan, on July 6, 2017. Hinged access panels are open on the spine of the fuselage over the main transmission shaft, on the forward pylon, under the engine nacelle, and on the sponson.

A Chinook helicopter being delivered to the 29th Combat Aviation Brigade is being offloaded from a US Air Force C-17 transport plane at Taji Military Complex, Iraq, on August 28, 2017, during the campaign to defeat ISIS in Iraq and Syria. The sides of the forward pylon are folded down, and the rotors have been removed and stored for transport.

Specialist Jedidiah Gaddie, US Army, a Chinook helicopter repairer from Company B, 628th Aviation Support Battalion, 28th Expeditionary Combat Aviation Brigade, is performing routine maintenance on a rotor of a Chinook helicopter in a hangar at a base in the Middle East on October 16, 2020. Next to his left hand is a blade drag damper.

A CH-47 Chinook helicopter from Company B, 3-10 General Support Aviation Brigade, takes off during the 10th Mountain Division's annual Exercise Mountain Peak at Fort Drum, New York, on October 23, 2016. *DVIDS*

This is the spectacular view from the cockpit of a South Carolina Army National Guard CH-47 while flying in support of the South Carolina Forestry Commission to fight a remote wildfire in the mountains in Pickens County, South Carolina, on November 17, 2016. *DVIDS*

A CH-47F Chinook, serial number 14-08162, assigned to Company B, 101st Combat Aviation Brigade, 101st Airborne Division (Air Assault), has touched down on a mountain in the Alps in Germany during an exercise on October 21, 2020. The insignia on the aft pylon depicts an elephant's head with white tusks.

A soldier is sitting on the partially lowered ramp of a CH-47F Chinook, serial number 07-08722, assigned to Company B, 3rd Battalion, 238th General Support Aviation Battalion, 28th Expeditionary Combat Aviation Brigade, during a hop over the desert to retrieve troops somewhere in the Middle East on November 11, 2020. The engines are equipped with Infrared Suppression System.

A Japanese Ground Self-Defense Force (JGSDF) Chinook helicopter assigned to the 1st Transport Helicopter Group, 1st Helicopter Brigade, is about to alight on the amphibious assault ship USS *America* (LHA-6) during a joint readiness exercise in the Philippine Sea on January 31, 2021. The CH-47J and improved CH-47JA were license-built by Kawasaki Heavy Industries in Japan.

A pair of petroleum supply specialists from the 3rd Battalion, 25th Aviation Regiment, 25th Combat Aviation Brigade, are refueling a Chinook at that regiment's area at Wheeler Army Airfield, Hawaii, on March 17, 2021. The NATO-standard D1 nozzle on the fuel hose is connected to a single-point-refueling receptacle inside a bay above the right forward landing-gear strut. The pressurized single-point fuel-filler system permits filling all fuel tanks, or selected ones, at a time.

In another photo taken at Wheeler Army Airfield on March 17, 2021, petroleum supply specialists from 3rd Battalion, 25th Aviation Regiment, are filling the left aft auxiliary fuel tank on this CH-47F, serial number 16-08472. Although the single-point system is the preferred one for refueling Chinooks, each fuel tank has a filler cap, for refueling them singly.

Mechanics with Company B, 602nd Aviation Support Battalion, 2nd Combat Aviation Brigade, are carefully inspecting a CH-47F Chinook in a hangar at Camp Humphreys, Republic of Korea, on March 3, 2022. The interior of the access door and the equipment bay in the front of the sponson are primed or painted a bright yellow, while the interiors of other access panels and doors are a yellowish green.

A pair of Chinook helicopters, including the CH-47F with serial number 04-08710 (*in the foreground*), assigned to the 185th Aviation Brigade, Mississippi Army National Guard, are about to land, to retrieve an Army unit during a proof-of-concept exercise at Camp Shelby Joint Forces Training Center, Mississippi, on April 29, 2022. On the closest CH-47F, the upper part of the ramp is retracted in the lower part.

Troops from the 1st Squadron, 98th Cavalry Regiment, 155th Armored Brigade Combat Team, Mississippi Army National Guard, are boarding CH-47F, serial number 04-08710, after finishing a proof of-concept exercise at Camp Shelby Joint Forces Training Center on April 29, 2022. On the side of the fuselage is a "towel bar" high-frequency radio antenna.

Two soldiers of the 3rd General Support Aviation Battalion, 25th Infantry Division, are on the top deck of a CH-47 Chinook to perform maintenance on the helicopter, parked on a flight line at Contingency Operating Base Speicher, Tikrit, Iraq, in 2016. Now, six decades after Boeing Vertol delivered the prototype YHC-1As to the Army, the CH-47 Chinooks are still proving their worth every day, around the world, and will likely do so well into the future. *DVIDS*